Active Lea with Aı

A Practical Guide

Stephen M. Kosslyn

ALINEA

Alinea
Learning Boston

ALINEA

Alinea Learning

Boston, Massachusetts

Published in the United States by Alinea Learning,

an imprint and division of Alinea Knowledge, LLC, Boston.

Library of Congress Cataloging-in-Publication Data is available on file.

Print book ISBN: 979-8-9892140-0-6

eBook ISBN: 979-8-9892140-1-3

Cover design by Imprudent Press LLC

Cover copyright © 2024 by Alinea Knowledge, LLC

Table of Contents

Preface

We are all educators. Some of us are teachers, some of us are professional course designers, some of us are parents—and some of us are lifelong learners, continuously educating ourselves. Some of us are all of the above. We are all facing an important moment in human history, with artificial intelligence (AI) poised to change every industry and, at the same time, promising to open up opportunities for every teacher and learner. Many of us are scrambling to catch up or strategizing to position ourselves to stay ahead of the changes. If we don't come to terms with AI, as individuals and as a society, there may be dire consequences for human flourishing and human freedom.

If you are an instructor or course designer, you'll need to quickly get up to speed on what AI can offer and figure out how to adapt to this new reality. This book is here to help you do that, and I'm pouring decades of experience into this—from being a dean at prestigious universities to launching groundbreaking entrepreneurial endeavors. Despite my decades of experience, including writing a book on neural networks three decades ago, I'm continually amazed at what's opening up in front of our eyes. AI is being used successfully to enhance teaching and learning all over the world, by people from large research institutions in the US to those at small training organizations in remote parts of Africa. This book is my attempt to take a complex subject and break it down for all of us, myself included, and share it as a tool that many can use to control their destiny.

I invite you to take on a "beginner's mind" with me, to keep your brain fresh and open as you engage with the ideas, methods, and practices I cover in this book. This book aims to help educators of all stripes to harness the latest, ground-breaking AI to design, deliver, and assess active learning. Grounded in many and varied research results, this book shows you how to use AI at every step of the way to apply scientifically validated principles of learning.

I did not intend to write this book. My initial idea was to write a second edition of my book *Active Learning Online: Five Principles that Make Online Courses Come Alive.* I wrote that book during the early phases of the Covid pandemic, and much was learned subsequently as instructors and learners gained more experience with online teaching and learning. This led me to revise the book to emphasize hybrid educational settings, which combine different in-person and online teaching modalities. I finished that revision in early 2023 and obtained reviews. One of the reviewers of my initial revision, John Katzman, prodded me to take a step back and consider how we can use AI to further active learning. His comment made me take pause, and I soon became convinced that these new AIs have profound implications for education—which led me to abandon the earlier revision and start a new one. Although I did retain some of the original version, particularly regarding the descriptions of each of the five principles of active learning, the current version diverged so far from the original that the publisher decided to release it as a separate book.

As in the earlier book on online learning, I've aimed for concision, stripping away anything not essential. I am guided, however, by a remark attributed to Abraham Lincoln—who, when asked, "How long should a man's legs be?" replied, "Long enough to reach the ground." When considering how long this book should be, in the same spirit, I've tried to make it just long enough to convey the essential content.

About the Author

Stephen M. Kosslyn is the Founder and President of Active Learning Sciences, Inc. He was the Founder, CEO, and then Chief Academic Officer of Foundry College. Prior to that, he was the Founding Dean and Chief Academic Officer of the Minerva Schools at the Keck Graduate Institute (now the fully accredited Minerva University). He previously served as Director of the Center for Advanced Study in the Behavioral Sciences and Professor of Psychology at Stanford University after having spent three decades on the faculty of Harvard University, serving as chair of the Department of Psychology, Dean of Social Science, and the John Lindsley Professor of Psychology. While at Harvard, he was also co-director of the Mind of the Market Lab at Harvard Business School and a member of the Department of Neurology at the Massachusetts General Hospital. He received a B.A. from UCLA and a Ph.D. from Stanford University, both in psychology. Kosslyn's research focuses on the science of learning, the nature of visual cognition, and visual communication. He has authored or co-authored 14 books and over 350 published papers on these topics. Kosslyn has received numerous honors, including the National Academy of Sciences Initiatives in Research Award, a Guggenheim Fellowship, three honorary Doctorates (University of Caen, University of Paris Descartes, Bern University), and election to the American Academy of Arts and Sciences.

—1—

Active Learning and AI

The Silicon Valley company OpenAI released its groundbreaking ChatGPT artificial intelligence (AI) software system on November 30th, 2022.[1] ChatGPT was trained to anticipate successive words or parts of words in an enormous number of documents, and it automatically abstracted patterns in this material. The system was then tuned up by humans, who reinforced desirable outputs and dampened down undesirable ones. All of this training enabled ChatGPT to respond to questions and requests. And its responses are often sophisticated and surprising. For example, it not only summarizes articles, but also critiques them. It not only drafts essays and emails, but also does so at a requested level of detail and in a requested style, such as formal, conversational, or casual. It not only provides feedback on an argument, it also revises it for you. It not only provides examples of specific concepts or situations, it also comes up with ideas on a large range of issues, from the details of how to structure a contract or business plan, to names for your club, to plot concepts for a novel. It is nothing short of amazing!

---

[1] The "G" stands for "Generative," the "P" for "Pretrained," and the "T" for Transformer, which relates to the specific method used to code input.

ChatGPT is an example of a particular type of AI known as *generative AI*. It creates new things rather than simply regurgitating what it previously stored. The initial generative AI systems fall into two main categories: Some—like ChatGPT—accept text as input and produce text as output. These programs are called "Large Language Models" (LLMs). LLMs are good at many things I had thought were safely in the realm of human specialization, notably creative and critical thinking.[2] And ChatGPT was just the beginning. OpenAI then released GPT-4, the fourth major revision of the software, which is even more powerful than its predecessor, and Google released its LLM, Bard, followed quickly by Meta's LLaMA (Large Language Model Meta AI), Anthropic's Claude, and LLMs from numerous other companies.

The other sort of initial generative AI, "Generative Image Models" (GIMs), deals with images. DALL-E, MidJourney, and Stable Diffusion are good examples of GIMs. Such software systems produce images based on descriptions, and these images can be nuanced and subtle. For example, if you ask for an image of a "depressed radish," you will get numerous examples of the dysphoric vegetable in various poses—some of which are remarkably evocative. Moreover, if you ask it to create images in a particular style, such as impressionist or cartoon, the GIM will accommodate.

It wasn't long before the two types of generative AIs began to merge. Some LLMs became capable of both accepting images as input and producing them as output. Moreover, the LLMs gained the ability to speak and interpret spoken language. New AIs will expand this multimodal capacity and be able to interpret and produce a wide variety of sounds as well as video. And every new feature opens up huge opportunities for innovation. Generative AI is new and exciting, and enables many novel

---

[2] For example, see Mollick, E. (2023, 13 August), Automating creativity. https://www.oneusefulthing.org/p/automating-creativity?utm_source=substack&utm_medium=email

and effective ways to teach. This is why we will focus on it in this book. In the remainder of this book I will refer to generative AIs simply as "AIs."

Shortly after the first LLMs appeared, many educators recognized educational uses of this technology, and we quickly saw LLM-based tutorial systems such as "Khanmigo," developed by the Khan Academy. But, somewhat surprisingly, no one focused on how to use these AIs systematically to design, deliver, and assess active learning. In active learning, learners engage in activities (such as debates or role-playing games) designed to help them grasp, acquire, or apply specific skills or knowledge. Active learning is in contrast to passive learning, such as occurs when learners simply listen to a lecture or watch a video. To be sure, some instructors and course designers offered ways to employ this new technology to administer bits and pieces of active learning,[3] but no one proposed an overarching, systematic approach to integrating AI into active learning.

This book fills that gap. It provides a principled approach to deploying the new AIs to design, deliver, and assess active learning. As such, this book offers a springboard for instructors and course designers—in middle school through graduate school and in the corporate world—by showing how to draw on AI to leverage decades of knowledge about how people learn, and thereby help your learners to succeed. This book is for both novice and highly experienced instructors and course designers who may not be deeply familiar with the science of learning or AI. It provides tools that enable you to employ AI to help learners acquire skills and knowledge more deeply and easily—and to make the process engaging and enjoyable.

This book also shows how incorporating AI into active learning opens the door to a new way to structure courses. This new learning modality

---

[3] Mollick, E. (2023, 1 February). The machines of mastery. https://www.oneusefulthing.org/p/the-machines-of-mastery. Mollick, E. R., & Mollick, L. (2023, 17 March). Using AI to implement effective teaching strategies in classrooms: Five strategies, including prompts. https://ssrn.com/abstract=4391243 or http://dx.doi.org/10.2139/ssrn.4391243

blurs the line between asynchronous (self-paced, individual) and synchronous (in real time, group) courses. This modality draws on the best of both formats while circumventing many of their weaknesses. Asynchronous courses are convenient, can effectively deliver content, and scale well, but are not good at providing active learning because learners do not receive effective, real-time feedback. In contrast, synchronous courses can provide effective active learning with real-time feedback, but they are rigidly scheduled and don't scale well. AI allows us to create a new type of course where we use a Learning Management System—such as Canvas, Blackboard, or Moodle—for content delivery, as in asynchronous courses, and use an AI for live active learning, as in synchronous courses. During active learning, the AI can perform many of the functions of engaged peers and an attentive, perceptive instructor, providing feedback and stimulating learners to think. This new sort of hybrid course offers a way to provide a high quality education that is convenient, inexpensive and easy to scale.

AI can help you at every phase of situating active learning in your courses. In particular, AI can help you:

- formulate learning objectives
- create syllabi
- organize individual class sessions
- select relevant readings (but these must be carefully checked)
- create assignments
- design active learning exercises that address a specific learning objective
- deliver active learning exercises that engage learners
- grade work products
- assess how much learners really know

For example, an AI can help you convert topics and subjects into specific learning objectives, which—as we shall see shortly—are an essential first step to devising effective active learning. To illustrate, I asked GPT-4 to do just this, using the following prompt. A "prompt" is an instruction or request to an AI. You can see below that it handled this request well.

Me:

Here are some academic subjects: "AI and active learning," "Online education," and "learning objective." Please convert these topics into learning objectives without using the verbs "understand," "learn," or "explore." Please make the learning objectives short and crisp.

AI:

Sure, here are the academic subjects converted into short and crisp learning objectives without using the verbs "understand," "learn," or "explore":

1. AI and active learning
    - Learning Objective: Assess the role of AI in enhancing active learning techniques.
2. Online education
    - Learning Objective: Evaluate the effectiveness of various online education strategies.
3. Learning objective
    - Learning Objective: Formulate clear and measurable learning objectives for diverse subjects.

However, I need to add a crucial caveat right up front: Results like this are not hard and fast. These new AIs are "generative"—instead of simply looking up and retrieving stored information, they generate it, producing something new. The inner workings of generative AIs incorporate a degree of randomness.[4] Thus, if you submit this prompt, you are not likely to get the exact same response that I did above. Indeed, even when the same person submits the same prompt repeatedly, they get at least slightly different results. For example, here's what I got when I submitted the identical prompt again to GPT-4:

---

[4] See Wolfram, S. (2023, 14 February). What is ChatGPT doing…and why does it work? *Stephen Wolfram Writings*: https://writings.stephenwolfram.com/2023/02/what-is-chatgpt-doing-and-why-does-it-work/

1. AI and active learning
   - Learning Objective: Apply AI techniques to enhance active learning strategies in diverse educational contexts.
2. Online education
   - Learning Objective: Design and implement effective online educational experiences for diverse learners.
3. Learning objective
   - Learning Objective: Formulate clear, measurable, and concise learning objectives for various instructional scenarios.

The results from a given prompt can also vary for other reasons. Notably, all of the AIs are continually being updated, and these changes can alter their performance in unexpected ways.[5] Furthermore, different AIs were trained on different materials and were "tuned" differently, which also affects their performance. I used GPT-4 for this book during the summer and fall of 2023. Hence, some of the prompts I offer may not work well by the time you submit them. In general, you need to run a prompt immediately before you give it to learners, and ensure that it works properly. (If you are interested in the specific prompts provided in this book, please visit www.activelearningsciences.com/prompts/; we will update the prompts regularly and post the current versions there.)

Recognizing these issues is the first step to resolving them. You can almost always adjust a prompt and get it to work. For example, in setting up an interactive activity, such as a debate, you need to instruct the AI to wait for the learner's response and then to address that response. However, sometimes the AI doesn't wait, but instead supplies a plausible response that a learner might make and then continues on, never giving the learner a chance to respond. You can address such problems simply by modifying the prompt to tell the AI what *not* to do—in this case, not to respond as if it were the learner, but instead to wait for the actual learner to respond before continuing. This is an easy fix, but they are not always

---

[5] Chen, L., Zaharia, M., & Zou, J. (2023, 1 August). *How is ChatGPT's behavior changing over time?* https://arxiv.org/pdf/2307.09009.pdf

so clear. In difficult cases, you can ask the AI to help you adjust a prompt so that it achieves your stated goal, and the AI is often remarkably helpful.

To be clear, these sorts of issues do not undermine the point of this book. My goal is not to give you prompts that you can plug and play. Rather, my aim is to give you a wide range of techniques you can employ with AI to design, deliver, and assess active learning. You can implement each of these techniques in many different ways, with many different prompts. I present each prompt and AI response to illustrate a basic idea; once you get the idea, you can exploit it in many ways. In the spirit of active learning, I invite you to try the prompts I provide and adjust them until you get something you can use for your own purposes.

Because this book is centered on the principles of active learning and how to use them, the subject matter will not go out of date as AIs become increasingly powerful. To the contrary, more capable AIs simply give you additional ways to implement the techniques we discuss here. Moreover, it's worth noting that as new features are added, the AIs are unlikely to lose their current abilities. They will continue to be able to help you design, deliver, and assess active learning in the ways I describe in this book.

What is Active Learning?

This book focuses not on AI in general but rather on its use in active learning. Why active learning? Simply put, because active learning is more effective than traditional teaching methods. For example, here are conclusions from a now-classic meta-analysis of 225 studies that compared active learning to traditional teaching methods in STEM (Science, Technology, Engineering, and Math) fields:

> ...The studies analyzed here document that active learning leads to increases in examination performance that would raise average grades by half a letter and that failure rates under traditional lecturing increase by 55% over the rates observed under active learning...Finally, the data suggest that STEM instructors may begin to question the continued use of traditional lecturing in everyday practice, especially in light of recent work indicating that active learning confers disproportionate benefits for STEM students from disadvantaged

backgrounds and for female students in male-dominated fields…[6]

Additional research has documented that the advantages of active learning apply beyond STEM fields. Active learning leads to better outcomes across the board. In a wide range of fields, active learning improves how well learners grasp, retain, and apply material.[7]

But what exactly is "active learning"? In a nutshell, active learning occurs when a person *uses knowledge or skills in the service of achieving a learning objective*. Learning objectives specify the goals for what should be learned. Each learning objective should lead to a specific *learning outcome*, the actual learning that is achieved. We need to design each active learning exercise to engage learners in material that will help them achieve a specific learning objective.[8]

---

[6] Freeman, S., Eddy, S. L., McDonough, M., Smith, M. K., Okoroafor, N., Jordt, H., & Wenderoth, M. P. (2014). Active learning increases student performance in science, engineering, and mathematics. *Proceedings of the National Academy of Sciences*, 111, 8410-8415. See also Michael, J. (2006). Where's the evidence that active learning works? *American Journal of Physiology - Advances in Physiology Education, 30,* 159-167. doi:10.1152/advan.00053.2006; Wieman, C. E. (2014). Large-scale comparison of science teaching methods sends clear message. *Proceedings of the National Academy of Sciences, 111*, 8319-8320; Wieman, C. (2017). *Improving how universities teach science: Lessons from the science education initiative*. Cambridge, MA: Harvard University Press

[7] Ambrose, S.A., Bridges, M.W., DiPietro, M., Lovett, M.C., Norman, M.K., & Mayer, R.E. (2010). *How learning works: Seven research-based principles for smart teaching*. San Francisco: Jossey-Bass; Bonwell, C. C., & Eison, J.A. (1991). *Active learning: Creating excitement in the classroom.* ASHE- ERIC Higher Education Report No. 1, Washington, D.C.: The George Washington University, School of Education and Human Development; Mello, D., & Less, C. A. (2013). Effectiveness of active learning in the arts and sciences. *Johnson & Wales University: Humanities Department Faculty Publications & Research. Paper 45.* http://scholarsarchive.jwu.edu/humanities_fac/45; Teagle Foundation (2016). *Promoting active learning in the humanities.* http://www.teaglefoundation.org/ Impacts-Outcomes/Project-Profile/Profiles/Creating-Sustained-Change-in-Practices-of-Engaged

[8] For similar, but not identical treatments, see Bonwell, C. C., & Eison, J.A. (1991). *Active learning: Creating excitement in the classroom*. ASHE-ERIC Higher Education Report No. 1, Washington, D.C.: The George Washington University, School of Education and Human Development; "Active Learning" in *Wikipedia*; https://en.wikipedia.org/wiki/Active_learning

Researchers, course designers, and instructors employ the term "active learning" in many ways,[9] so let me be clear on what I mean by it here: When I refer to active learning, I mean *learning by using*. This is not the same as the common characterization of *learning by doing*. In learning by using, the instructor initially presents content that learners must grasp in order to achieve a learning objective. But learners won't absorb much content simply by passively listening or watching. Rather, after the initial exposure, they need to *use* the content in some way. For instance, they can use it to prepare for a debate with an AI, to record a podcast that explains the material, or to solve specific problems. The learners should use the content in a way that will help them achieve the learning objective—and thus, the nature of the activity itself is determined in part by the learning objective.

In contrast, "learning by doing" also includes activities such as open-ended discussions, discovery learning, exploration-based learning, inquiry-based learning, and experiential learning. Such activities rarely are designed with a specific learning objective in mind, and such unstructured activities are rarely effective means of learning.[10] However, we can convert many of these sorts of activities to "learning by using" by starting with a learning objective, providing appropriate background, and designing the activity to address the learning objective.

Most instructors and course designers already draw on some active learning, if only by posing reflection questions, presenting polls, or requiring learners to take spot quizzes. Such activities are a start, but they do not take full advantage of what you can accomplish with in-depth active

---

[9] Lombardi, D., Shipley, T. F., Bailey, J. M., Bretones, P. S., Prather, E. E., Ballen, C. J., Knight, J. K., Smith, M. K., Stowe, R. L., Cooper, M. M., Prince, M., Atit, K., Uttal, D. H., LaDue, N. D., McNeal, P. M., Ryker, K., St. John, K., van der Hoeven Kraft, K. J., & Docktor, J. L. (2021). The curious construct of active learning. *Psychological Science in the Public Interest, 22*, 8–43. https://doi.org/10.1177/1529100620973974

[10] Kirschner, P.A., Sweller, J., & Clark, R. E. (2006). Why minimal guidance during instruction does not work: An analysis of the failure of constructivist, discovery, problem-based, experiential, and inquiry-based teaching. *Educational Psychologist, 41:2*, 75-86, DOI: 10.1207/s15326985ep4102_1; Mayer, R. E. (2004). Should there be a three-strikes rule against pure discovery learning? The case for guided methods of instruction. *American Psychologist, 59*, 14-19.

learning, especially—as we shall see—active learning with AI. To take full advantage of active learning, the instructor or course designer needs a well-defined learning objective and must structure the activity so that it helps learners to achieve that objective. A well-defined learning objective, such as those the AI produced above, is *specific*, *concrete*, and produces *measurable results*. Active verbs introduce these sorts of learning objectives, including: summarize, identify, describe, analyze, define, explain, evaluate, apply, demonstrate, predict, and create. If a learning objective does not utilize a verb like one of these, we will not be able to deploy it effectively. For example, verbs such as "understand," "learn," or "explore" are not specific or concrete and do not imply measurable results. And thus we will not be able to easily decide whether learners have, in fact, understood, learned, or explored something—to what depth, for how long? We can address these goals much more effectively by formulating learning objectives that rely on more specific, concrete and measurable verbs.

Active learning can be entirely self-directed, such as when you use information you glean from a book or video to accomplish a task. For example, you might watch a YouTube video to figure out how to get your toilet to flush properly, and then use that information to solve the problem, or you might rely on a cookbook to guide you in preparing a new dish, and so on. In such cases, you define the learning objective, access the relevant content, and use that content in an activity. Although the principles we discuss in this book apply equally well to such self-directed learning as to active learning with AI, we will focus on the latter in order to make your classes more effective, engaging and enjoyable.

How to Use This Book

This book is intended for instructors and course designers in many contexts. This is a broad and varied group, and different readers may have different goals. You can read and use this book in three different ways, depending on your goals.

First, if you are preparing to teach a course or classes, you can read this book to help you direct an AI to design, deliver, and assess active learning. If that's your goal, I recommend reading the book straight through—the chapters are ordered to facilitate this use. However, at the end of each chapter, I recommend pausing to play with the prompts in your preferred AI, and adapting them to your own purposes. Not only will this practice help you learn the material ("learning by using"), but it will also allow you to come up for air—there's a lot here.

Second, if you are interested primarily in how to apply the science of learning to education, you can read this book to see how to leverage the learning principles with AI. If that's your goal, you probably should read Chapters 2 and 3 and then read the rest in any order that interests you— and you might want to skim over the boxed material, given that the specifics of what the AI did may not be of great interest.

And third, if you are interested primarily in general ideas about how to use AI in education, you can read Chapter 2 and then dip into the following chapters in any order. You may want to focus on the boxes in the chapters, the material in the text that introduces the boxes, the sections at the end of each chapter, and Chapter 11.

A Quick Overview of What Is to Come

The remainder of the book contains the following chapters:

Chapter 2. Using AI in Active Learning. We can easily use AI to help us with all phases of designing, delivering, and assessing active learning. We here review the advantages of using AI in these ways, and then consider a detailed example: using AI to conduct a debate. We then examine limitations of AI, and the crucial roles that humans must play when using them in education. You can circumvent or minimize many of the limitations of AI by creating appropriate prompts. Thus, we conclude by considering how to design prompts to lead the AI to do what you want it to do.

Chapter 3. The Science of Learning. This book is evidence-based; it is rooted in key facts about cognitive functioning. These facts provide the foundations for the principles at the core of the book. In particular, in this chapter, we review the relationships between "learning" and "memory" and consider the roles of several different types of "memory stores" that exist in the human brain. We also examine the processes that underlie different phases of learning—from organizing and interpreting what we encounter, to storing and retaining it, to later retrieving it. These are the foundations of the five principles that underlie all active learning. These principles, in turn, drive the way we employ AI to design, deliver, and assess active learning.

Chapter 4. Deep Processing. This is the first of five chapters that each summarize one of the principles of the science of learning.[11] The key idea captured by this first principle is that the more a person mentally processes information, the more likely it is that the person will learn it. This principle leads us to lead learners to pay attention to and think through material that addresses the learning objective. The Principle of Deep Processing lies at the core of all active learning, and thus we begin with it as a foundation. In this and the following four chapters, we consider how to use AI to induce learners to engage in one particular type of mental processing—and see examples of prompts that elicit such processing. Asking AI to create active learning exercises based on only a single learning principle results in a wide range of specific activities. Like humans, AIs can be more creative when they must work within specific constraints.[12]

Chapter 5. Chunking. People can only take in about three or four organized units of information, "chunks," at the same time. Thus, minimizing the number of chunks while teaching is critical. Chunking—the process of organizing material into units—applies to all forms of

---

[11] I have organized the relevant literature into five principles in an effort to be clear and concise, with an eye toward formulating the principles so that they can be most usefully applied to teaching and learning. Other researchers have proposed alternative organizations—but it is all the same material, just organized differently. For example, see Graesser, A.C., Halpern, D.F., & Hakel, M. (2008). *25 principles of learning*. Washington, DC: Task Force on Lifelong Learning at Work and at Home. (For a summary, see Graesser, A.C., (2009). *Journal of Educational Psychology, 101*, 259-261.); Willingham, D. T. (2009). *Why don't students like school? A cognitive scientist answers questions about how the mind works and what it means for the classroom*. San Francisco, CA: Wiley/Jossey-Bass

[12] Finke, R. A., Ward, T. B., & Smith, S. M. (1992). *Creative cognition: Theory, research, and applications*. Cambridge, MA: MIT Press.

information, ranging from perceptual (e.g., visual, auditory), to conceptual (e.g., different factors that produce a condition or situation, such as global warming), to skills (e.g., those required to play a sport). In this chapter, we see how AI can help chunk material and can teach the rules that underlie various forms of chunking.

Chapter 6. Building Associations. Mental associations play a crucial role in organizing and interpreting information when it is first encountered, in integrating information into what is already known so that it is retained well, and in providing cues that allow you to dig information out of your memory stores when you need it. In this chapter, we see how to use AI to elicit and create such associations, and how associations help to solve the greatest single problem in the science of learning: the problem of transfer, of applying information learned in one context (such as in class) to other contexts (such as situations at work and in daily life).

Chapter 7. Dual Coding. Learning and memory are more effective when information is presented in multiple modalities, such as visually and verbally: showing and telling is better than either perceptual or verbal modes alone. This principle reflects the fact that our brains have multiple different memory stores, and we learn information better when it is entered into more than one such store. We see how the image interpretation and image production capabilities of AIs can help implement this principle in multiple ways.

Chapter 8. Deliberate Practice. Deliberate practice is not just doing the same thing over and over. Rather, deliberate practice requires using feedback to identify the most difficult (for each specific learner) aspects of what is being learned and then devoting proportionally more time and effort to mastering those aspects. Perhaps counterintuitively, learning is best when learners make errors, which allow them to identify where to focus their efforts. This chapter explains and illustrates the advantages of using AI to design and deliver activities that engender deliberate practice.

Chapter 9. Combining Principles. Although we can draw on each of the principles individually, they gain force when combined. We here consider a range of practices, from the power of testing to the use of mnemonics to gamification, and we see how AI can design and deliver active learning exercises that draw on combinations of the principles and thereby enhance learning.

Chapter 10. Intrinsic and Extrinsic Motivation. The principles of the science of learning make a difference only when learners participate and are engaged in an activity. This chapter discusses ways to motivate learners based on theories of intrinsic motivation and theories of extrinsic motivation. We consider how to bake such motivational factors into active learning with AI.

Chapter 11. Creating, Situating, and Evaluating. We conclude by putting active learning in context. We first review many examples of specific types of active learning, and consider prompts that will help you to employ AI to design and deliver different activities. These examples and prompts are a starting place that will help you use active learning with AI effectively in every class. We then review how to structure a class session to exploit active learning and how to create rubrics that will allow you to assess what learners have actually learned.

—2—

Using AI in Active Learning

We just saw that instructors have employed active learning successfully for decades. Why fix what's not broken? Even though traditional active learning is highly effective, there is room for improvement. In particular, traditional active learning is often very labor-intensive, logistically challenging, and difficult to scale. As we see in this chapter, when properly deployed, AI can make a good thing even better. In what follows, we first consider reasons for using AI to design, deliver, and assess active learning, and then review different ways that AI can interact with learners. We then see a detailed example of a complex "social" interaction with an AI, which guides learners to use material that underlies a specific learning objective. We then turn to limitations of using AI in active learning, and education more broadly, and underscore the critical role of the humans who work with AIs. As we see, we can obviate many of the potential problems with AI, at least in part, by submitting appropriate prompts. Thus, we conclude with a discussion of how to create prompts.

How AI Can Improve Active Learning

An AI can help you design, deliver, and assess numerous sorts of active learning, many of which are difficult to achieve without it. The advantages of using AI in active learning include the following.

Designing Activities

AI allows you to personalize active learning. Notably:

- AI can design active learning exercises that are easily adjusted to fit each individual learner's level of knowledge, skill, and learning speed.

- AI can easily craft active learning exercises around each learner's particular interests.

- AI can create active learning exercises that allow each individual learner to ask follow-up questions and discuss material of particular interest.

More generally, AI can help you carry out key steps in designing active learning exercises. For example:

- AI can help you create learning objectives quickly and easily based on descriptions of subjects or topics.

- AI can design active learning exercises quickly and easily to address specific learning objectives.

- AI can design a very large number of types of active learning exercises quickly and easily (see Chapter 11).

Delivering Activities

AI can deliver active learning exercises effectively and efficiently. Specifically:

- AI allows you to deploy active learning inexpensively at scale.

- AI allows you to easily deploy active learning in many situations where it is logistically difficult to deploy traditional active learning.

- AI allows learners to engage in interactive active learning at a convenient time and place, and they can take as long as they need to complete it.

Assessing Activities

AI can assess active learning exercises in principled and informative ways. Specifically:

- AI can easily create rubrics that specify objective criteria for evaluating work products, which can reduce the effects of many forms of bias (e.g., gender, age, or race).

- AI can use rubrics to automatically assess work products created during active learning, rapidly providing specific feedback to each learner.

- AI can utilize rubrics flexibly and automatically to assess many different sorts of evidence of learning, ranging from a piece of writing to remarks made in a discussion.

- AI can create and deliver questions and various types of assignments to assess how well each learner has mastered the material.

You can use the new AIs in two general ways to capitalize on these advantages. One way is to have the AI design an activity in advance that is later delivered to the learners off-line. For example, you can deliver the activity via a Learning Management System in an asynchronous course. After the learners complete the activity, you can have the AI evaluate their work products and quickly provide feedback. An advantage of this type of activity is that you have complete control over exactly what the learners will do; you can run the prompt multiple times and select the variant of the activity that you like best, and edit it as you see fit.

The other way to leverage the advantages of using AI for active learning requires learners to have multiple, dynamic interactions with the AI over the course of an active learning exercise, such as occurs in a role-playing game, debate, or interview. Following this, in the same session, the AI can assess the learners' performance and provide feedback.

In this second type of exercises, the AI will probably provide a different variant of the exercise each time the prompt is submitted. This can work to your advantage: As we see in Chapter 10, it is good to give learners some choice. You can allow learners to submit a prompt for this sort of interactive exercise several times, and let them engage with a version they find inviting. It's easy to write instructions for learners that apply to all variants of a given type of activity, even though the details of the activity may vary each time it is implemented. For example, if the activity is a debate, the instructions will apply regardless of the details of the content, and the same is true if the activity is a particular type of problem-solving exercise, designing a Mind Map, drafting a story, and so on.

In this book we primarily consider examples of the second approach. This is the most novel use of AI and potentially the most powerful. This sort of interaction can be lively, engaging, and stimulating, and can effectively draw on the learning principles we will review in this book.

An Example: Using AI to Conduct a Debate

To make all of this concrete, let's now consider a detailed example of active learning with AI, using a highly interactive exercise. In this case, the learning objective is "Identify the pros and cons of laws that fund elections publicly." One way you, the instructor or course designer, can employ active learning to help learners achieve a learning objective is to organize a debate with the AI. Here's an example of how this would work:

1. You want learners to "identify the pros and cons of laws that fund elections publicly," so the activity should lead them to use relevant material they've received about the benefits and drawbacks of publicly funding elections. You design a debate where learners will address the proposition, "Laws should be passed to fund elections publicly."

2. You send instructions and a prompt to learners and ask them to read the instructions, then enter the prompt into the AI, and

then interact appropriately.[13] The instructions focus on the learning objective and the form of the activity. The AI may vary the details of the activity whenever the prompt is submitted, but the form should adhere to what you put in the prompt.

In this example, you send the following instructions and prompt:

Instructions to the Learner

You should begin by asking the AI questions in order to build the best case you can for both sides of the debate. You will soon be assigned to argue either the pro or the con side, but you won't know in advance which side you will be assigned. The mere fact of preparing for both sides of a debate is a form of active learning which will help you to master the material. Ask the AI about both positions until you are comfortable with them. When you are ready, please tell the AI that you are ready for the debate. The AI will begin by providing an argument about the proposition. In response, you should provide a counterargument to whatever the AI asserts. Please record the strongest and weakest arguments made by the AI, and explain why you made these judgments; you will need to turn in this list and your evaluations at the end.

AI Prompt

You[14] will play the role of an instructor who is trying to help a student achieve the following learning objective: "Identify the pros and cons of laws that fund elections publicly." As the first step, you will ask the human student to ask you questions about this topic. Before continuing, wait for the student to type in a question. Then answer the question to help the student to build the cases for both the pro and con sides of this proposition:

---

[13] In this book I've described the most direct way to interact with the AI, which requires no additional tools or software. However, we have developed software that automates this process, which simplifies both administering and participating in active learning exercises. This software allows a Learning Management System to submit prompts and background material to an AI without showing them to the learners (for information on the software, contact info@activelearningsciences.com).

[14] Note: The "you" here refers to the AI: the prompt is telling it what to do.

"Laws should be passed to fund elections publicly." Be sure to provide a balanced case. When the student is ready, they will tell you that they are ready to debate. When the student so indicates, choose one side at random—"pro" or "con"—and tell the student that they will take that side, and you will begin the debate with an argument for the other side. You then begin the debate by taking your side, whichever it is, and providing a good argument for that position. The student will counter with an argument for the other side, and you will provide a counterargument to support your side. Have four exchanges, and then thank the student for a stimulating debate.

As you can see in Box 1, the prompt worked well, and the learner and AI had a productive debate. The debate led the learner to draw on knowledge that directly addresses the learning objective—even though the learner may have thought that the AI was doing all the work! The detailed transcript of the AI's responses are in a box because the specific responses are less important than the general point, which is to illustrate how you can deploy an AI to facilitate active learning.

BOX 1: Using AI to conduct a debate
(After the prompt is submitted)

AI:
Please feel free to ask any questions you have about the pros and cons of laws that fund elections publicly. I'm here to help you understand the topic better and build your case for both sides.

Me (Learner):
Can you please give me an overview of the pro and con positions?

AI:
Of course! I'll provide a brief overview of the pro and con positions on laws that fund elections publicly.

<u>Pros:</u>

1. Reduces the influence of money in politics: Publicly funded elections can reduce the dependence of candidates on private donors, diminishing the potential for corruption and influence peddling.
2. Encourages a more diverse range of candidates: With financial barriers lowered, more individuals from various backgrounds may be encouraged to run for office, resulting in a more diverse and representative government.
3. Levels the playing field: Public funding can help level the playing field between well-funded and less-funded candidates, enabling a fairer competition based on ideas and policies rather than financial resources.
4. Increases transparency: Public funding systems usually have strict reporting requirements, which can make campaign financing more transparent and easier to monitor.

Cons:
1. Cost to taxpayers: Publicly funded elections require taxpayer money, which could be allocated to other pressing needs or result in increased taxes.
2. Free speech concerns: Some argue that limiting private campaign contributions infringes on free speech rights, as individuals and organizations may want to express their political views through financial support.
3. Inefficient allocation of resources: Public funding may not always be distributed fairly or effectively, potentially benefiting undeserving candidates or disadvantaging those who need the funds most.
4. May not eliminate private influence: Even with public funding, candidates may still seek out private donations or engage with special interest groups, so the influence of money in politics may not be entirely eliminated.

Feel free to ask more questions or seek clarification on any points. When you're ready to begin the debate, just let me know!

Me (Learner):
That's great! OK, I think I'm ready for the debate.

AI:

Great! I have randomly chosen a side for you, and you will be arguing for the "pro" position in favor of laws that fund elections publicly. I will argue the "con" side.

To begin, I'll present an argument against publicly funded elections: One major concern with publicly funded elections is the cost to taxpayers. Funding elections through public money would require additional government expenditure, which could be better allocated to other pressing needs such as healthcare, education, or infrastructure. Furthermore, it might lead to increased taxes, placing an additional burden on taxpayers.

Now it's your turn to present an argument in favor of publicly funded elections.

Me (Learner):
It makes the system simpler and more transparent.

AI:
That's a valid point. Publicly funded elections can indeed simplify the campaign finance system and increase transparency, as candidates would be less reliant on private donations, and the funding process would be subject to stricter reporting requirements and government oversight.

However, it's important to consider that even with public funding, candidates may still be motivated to seek out private donations or engage with special interest groups to gain an advantage over their competitors. This means that the influence of money in politics may not be entirely eliminated, and issues of transparency and fairness might still persist.

Now, please present another argument in favor of publicly funded elections.

Me (Learner):
First, let me note that we can simply outlaw private funding if we adopt public funding. Second, this system would produce a more representative set of candidates.

AI:
You raise some valid points. Outlawing private funding could potentially reduce the influence of money in politics and lead to a more transparent system. Additionally, publicly funded elections could indeed encourage a more diverse range of candidates. By lowering financial barriers to entry, individuals from various socio-economic backgrounds would be more likely to participate in the political process. This could result in a government that is more representative of the population.

However, it's important to consider the potential free speech concerns associated with limiting private campaign contributions. Some argue that restricting individuals and organizations from financially supporting candidates could be seen as an infringement on their right to express their political views.

Please share another argument in favor of publicly funded elections.

Me (Learner):
Publicly funded elections would keep overall costs from spiraling out of control, as is happening now.

AI:
That's a good point. Publicly funded elections can help control campaign spending by establishing limits on the amount of money candidates can receive and spend. This can prevent the escalation of campaign costs, reduce the pressure on candidates to constantly fundraise, and help focus their attention on policy issues and engaging with voters. However, one concern related to controlling campaign spending through public funding is the potential for inefficient allocation of resources. It might be challenging to ensure that funds are distributed fairly and effectively among candidates, with some potentially receiving more than they need or deserve, while others might struggle to access the resources necessary for their campaigns.

Now, please present your final argument in favor of publicly funded elections.

Me (Learner):
Publicly funded elections would greatly curtail the power of special interests.

AI:
You're absolutely right. Publicly funded elections can indeed help reduce the influence of special interest groups on political campaigns. By providing candidates with a more reliable and less partisan source of funding, candidates may be less likely to rely on, and be influenced by, special interest groups and their agendas.

Nonetheless, it's important to acknowledge that publicly funded elections might not entirely eliminate the power of special interests. Some groups may still find ways to exert influence through indirect means, such as issue advocacy or funding political action committees (PACs) that support particular candidates or causes.

Thank you for a stimulating debate! It's crucial to consider various perspectives and weigh the pros and cons when discussing important issues like publicly funded elections. I hope this discussion has provided valuable insights and helped you better understand the topic.

3. You, as the instructor, ask the learners to turn in the transcripts of their interactions with the AI or to "share" them with you, using the button at the upper right on the screen of ChatGPT or GPT-4. You then feed them into the AI (either by cutting and pasting or using an "Application Programming Interface," an API) and ask it to determine whether any are identical. If they are, you've spotted cheating—a learner has simply submitted the transcript obtained by someone else. The randomness built into generative AI ensures that no two actual interactions will be exactly the same. Ideally, the AI also records video at the time of the interaction, which allows you to ensure that the appropriate learner was responding.

4. At this point, you ask the learners to turn in their observations of the strongest and weakest arguments made by the AI, along with the rationale for their evaluations.

However, in this example—and most of those in the remainder of this book—a potential problem is that the learners can try to avoid doing the work, and thereby not engage in active learning, by asking the AI to do the task for them. In this case, they would submit the transcript of the debate to an AI and ask it to summarize the strongest and weakest arguments and justify those evaluations. One way to circumvent this problem is to have the AI conduct a follow-up interview immediately after the debate. Only then would it ask the learner to provide their observations and explain or justify their responses. This procedure requires the learners to respond in real time to specific questions—and follow-up questions—that are difficult to anticipate in advance. Again, ideally, the AI would video this interaction.

5. Finally, you, the instructor, ask the AI to draw on a rubric to grade the learner's observations and evaluations (as illustrated in Chapter 11). However, you need to check the AI's grading to ensure accuracy, and edit appropriately, before sending the feedback to the learners. "Trust, but verify" not only applies to nuclear weapons negotiators, but also to AIs. Critically, all learners know from the outset that they will have a debrief after the debate, and hence should be motivated to pay close attention. The sequence of events is summarized in Figure 2.1.

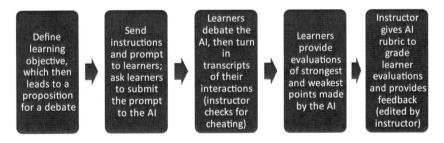

Figure 2.1. *The sequence of events in an AI-mediated debate.*

This sort of activity with an AI is a powerful way to promote learning. Perhaps counterintuitively, active learning can be effective even if learners are not trying to learn. The principles that underlie learning can be at work even if learners are unaware of them or not intentionally trying to achieve a specific learning outcome. The key is to design activities that lead learners *to use the knowledge or skills that underlie a learning objective.*

Indeed, this debate with an AI would induce active learning in several ways: First, because the learners have to ask the AI questions, they are not passively receiving information but rather are engaging with the material, processing it, and determining what additional information they need. Then, they use that information in the debate. Following this, they evaluate the debate and choose the strongest and weakest arguments. In short, the debate leads learners to pay attention and think through material that underlies the learning objective, which is the essence of the first principle we consider from the science of learning (in Chapter 4).

This example of using a debate with an AI to promote active learning also illustrates another aspect of such learning: Although it should be engaging and enjoyable for learners, it often requires more effort than if they were just sitting passively listening to a lecture or watching a video. This is important because researchers have found that learners may misinterpret the extra effort required in active learning as indicating that they don't learn as much as they would have learned from a lecture—even when the opposite is, in fact, true.[15] However, these same researchers found that most learners came to appreciate the effectiveness of active learning as the course progressed. In addition, you can enhance this feeling by regular assessments of their knowledge and feedback about their learning progress. These researchers also found that learners appreciated active learning more when the instructor preemptively struck, telling them at the outset that they will be working harder when they engage in active learning and that this will result in more, not less,

---

[15] Deslauriers, L., McCarty, L. S., Miller, K., Callaghan, K., & Kestin, G. (2019). Measuring actual learning versus feeling of learning in response to being actively engaged in the classroom. *Proceedings of the National Academy of Sciences, 116*, 19251-19257.

learning—which contradicts the belief that traditional teaching is more rigorous and thus induces more learning.

Limitations of Using AI in Active Learning

AI is so useful in designing, delivering, and assessing active learning that it might be easy to lose sight of its limitations. We need humans in the loop to try to circumvent and compensate for these limitations. This is a rapidly moving field, and hence AI developers should resolve many—if not most—of these limitations in the near future. Nevertheless, it's worth considering the implications of each of them. I've organized key limitations into three broad categories, and offer suggestions about how to address many of these limitations.

Cognitive and Interpretative Limitations

This set of limitations reflects AI's lack of genuine understanding or interpretation and its reliance on potentially biased, incomplete or outdated training data.

- *No real comprehension:* AIs, as marvelous as they are, don't really grasp the meaning, significance, or context of what they produce. Moreover, AIs sometimes are overly literal and their training data may lead them to misinterpret input. This is particularly a problem if the prompt is vague or ambiguous, and hence designing good prompts is crucial.

- *Limited training set:* Every AI was trained on a specific set of data, which may include biases or be an unrepresentative sample. In addition, AIs may not always be updated, and as a result their responses might be based on outdated information. These limitations can lead to many problems. For example, AIs can make errors when grading learners' work products without specific guidance. This is a good reason to give AIs relevant resources to draw on, and stress in the prompt that the AI should use those resources over other information it has. Moreover, you should also give the AI rubrics and instructions on how to use them in grading (see

Chapter 11).

- **"Hallucinations":** By their very nature, AIs act on inputs to complete patterns they abstracted during training. This can result in their producing incorrect information. For example, an AI may claim incorrectly that a person who received one honor for academic achievement also won several other similar honors. This is particularly a problem if AIs are used to answer questions. Although even a standard internet search can produce misinformation, AIs are often confident and convincing even when they present falsehoods. Hence, humans need to regard AI responses skeptically. However, you can go a long way toward minimizing hallucinations by providing background materials, such as relevant articles or chapters, and prompt the AI to base its responses on those resources. As of this writing, GPT-4 has a version that allows users to submit documents up to about 24,000 words long and Anthropic's Claude-2 AI allows users to submit up to about 75,000 words. This allows you to submit considerable amounts of background material along with your prompt.

- **Factor neglect:** An AI can overlook key factors, such as relevant variables when solving problems. When an AI makes such an error, simply revise the prompt to instruct it to pay attention to the relevant factors and try again.

- **Generalizing to novel, specialized, or nuanced content:** Because any given AI is limited by the set of data used to train it, it may have difficulty addressing novel, specialized, or nuanced content. For example, although AIs can usually solve physics problems that are included in standard textbooks, they falter when asked to solve novel, specialized, nuanced "real world" problems that probably were not in the training set. [16] Hence, when addressing such topics, you should

---

[16] Carl Wieman, (7 September 2023), personal communication. See also Wang, K. D., Burkholder, E., Wieman, C., Salehi, S., & Haber, N. (2023, 21 September). Examining the

submit relevant resources along with the prompt, and instruct the AI to draw on those resources when responding instead of using other information it has. You can submit the resources directly to the AIs if they fit within its input limitations, or, for some AIs, you can simply link to the resources.

- *Limited quantitative skills:* Generative AIs typically are not good at many types of math, and may make errors when given tasks that require quantitative skills. Supplementary systems ("Plug-ins"), such as Wolfram Alpha, may solve this problem by handling such tasks for AIs. But until this problem is clearly solved, it's best to be cautious when using generative AI for calculation-intensive tasks.

Interaction and Emotional Response Limitations

AIs also have limitations in how they interact with users, which result in part from their inability to experience emotions.

- *Responsive, not intentional:* AIs have no goals or intentions of their own; what AIs produce depends on how they are prompted. Humans must set clear goals and craft unambiguous and effective prompts—and then evaluate the results to determine whether they are appropriate.

- *No actual emotion:* AIs do not experience actual emotions. Although they sometimes may seem to try to act "human," they ultimately cannot do so—if only because they literally have no idea of what it's like to be a human. An AI's superficial mannerisms are just that: superficial. Learners should be aware of, and avoid being seduced by, such mannerisms.

- *No learner background:* AIs are not aware of each learner's personal circumstances or current state of mind. Learners should only expect AIs to respond to them as individuals

---

potential and pitfalls of ChatGPT in science and engineering problem-solving. Stanford University preprint.

based on specific information they provide, and should realize that AIs will not retain such information from session to session.

- *Privacy and security:* It is not clear how the AI companies use the data we produce when we interact with AIs. Thus, we must be cautious about including sensitive or private information when we interact with AIs.

Social and Societal Limitations

This category concerns how limitations of AI can have unintended consequences on human social behavior and society.

- *Reducing human interaction:* Although AIs are often highly engaging, they are not people and cannot substitute for human relationships. If we rely too much on AIs in education, we may undermine crucial aspects of social-emotional learning. This is particularly an issue with traditional-age college learners. Moreover, bonding with other humans can motivate learners to continue their studies. [17] At least for traditional-aged learners, if we rely too much on AIs, we risk undermining learner motivation.

- *Abdicating responsibility:* AIs are so effective, and likely to become even more effective over time, that course designers, instructors, and learners may become dependent on them and uncritically accept the educational materials they develop. But, as good as they are, they aren't perfect. Human instructors need to keep learning objectives in mind, ensure that educational materials do in fact address those learning objectives, monitor how learners are progressing, help them to overcome obstacles, and motivate them to continue.

---

[17] Hausmann, L.R.M., Schofield, J.W., & Woods, R.L. (2007). Sense of belonging as a predictor of intentions to persist among African American and White first-year college students. *Research in Higher Education, 48,* 803-839.

- ***Ethics:*** Complex and difficult ethical issues surround almost every aspect of AI. For example, AIs can provide damaging or dangerous information, ranging from false accusations about individuals to instructions on how to build bombs. In order to curtail such problems, AI companies use reinforcement learning from human feedback to create "guardrails" for AIs. However, such tuning may itself have unexpected consequences. Course designers and instructors should be aware of ethical issues, and be sensitive to their potential effects on learners.

- ***Increasing social disparities:*** Effective education with AI runs the risk of widening the gap between rich and poor. In order to have the chance to interact with AIs and reap their educational benefits, learners need access to the internet and computers, tablets, or smartphones—but many do not have access or such devices. Indeed, in some countries, simply having reliable electricity is a challenge. Such issues should be addressed by governments, NGOs, foundations, and companies.

Given all the potential pitfalls of using AI, we shouldn't be surprised that it's easy to trip it up and have it produce incorrect, misleading, or otherwise unsuitable products and responses. However, experiencing such a problem is not a reason to stop using AI. Rather, it is a reason to diagnose the problem, improve the prompt, perhaps submit resource materials, and try again. The goal is to figure out how to get an AI to do what we want it to do.

Despite the challenges, AI has enormous potential to help human learners succeed in their studies, especially when it is used to enhance active learning. But at every step, we need to bear in mind the limitations of AIs, and the fact that they are a way to augment human teaching, not replace it. This book provides many ways that we humans can use AIs constructively and productively, but we must be mindful of the limitations of AIs while at the same time taking advantage of what they do well.

Creating and Adapting Prompts

As we just saw, you can address many of the potential issues with using AI in active learning by creating appropriate prompts. When you develop new prompts or adapt existing ones when they do not produce the desired results, the following guidelines will help you get what you want. I based these guidelines on best practices and guidance from GPT-4. They are ordered roughly in terms of relative importance:

- *Iterative approach:* If the initial response from the AI isn't exactly what you are looking for, and in my experience, it rarely is, do the following: diagnose what the problem is, refine your prompt by drawing on the following specific recommendations, observe the results with the refined prompt, and modify the prompt again if need be. Keep iterating until you achieve your goal. At that point, ensure that you can deploy the prompt in the future by starting a new chat session and verifying that the prompt works as expected, even without the context of the previous interactions. GPT-4 and some other AIs include all previous prompts and responses in subsequent inputs during a single chat session, but do not store that information for future applications of the prompt. But even such double-checking is not enough: As noted earlier, you should try out AI-delivered active learning exercises right before you give them to learners.

- *Unambiguous for the AI:* Ensure that each prompt states the goal and specifies relevant information clearly and unambiguously—as interpreted by the AI. This is sometimes harder than it sounds, in part because the AI may interpret instructions in surprising ways. If you find it doing this, you can try telling it what you *don't* want it to do. We saw an example earlier where the AI responded for the learner rather than pausing to wait for the actual learner's responses. In addition, in other cases the AI initially produced not the activity itself but rather a summary of what the activity would be. In all such situations, you can usually fix the problem by telling the AI more clearly, often with examples, what to do and what not to do.

- **_Structured instructions:_** Simply adding "Let's think step by step" to the prompt can markedly improve how well AIs perform complex tasks.[18] For complex or multi-part prompts, you can facilitate such processing by organizing the prompt into a step-by-step structure. For example, if you want the AI first to deliver an activity and then to report on how well the learners performed it, you would first provide information about the activity itself and then follow that with instructions about how to evaluate the learners' performance. To ensure that the AI responds to each step or aspect of the activity, provide headings that concisely label each of them. In addition, repeating key information in the prompt helps to keep the AI on track. Some redundancy can go a long way. You will see examples of this in the pages that follow.

- **_Relevant background information:_** You may not need to provide much background information if you ask an AI to address material that many sources describe consistently and redundantly (such as material in textbooks). The AI was probably trained on such material, and can draw on the patterns it abstracted from them. However, to ensure that the results are accurate, and not hallucinations, submit relevant source materials or a link to them—and instruct the AI to base its responses on these materials. For example, you can submit specific articles or link to encyclopedia pages. In addition, you can include background directly in the prompt. For instance, when asking the AI to develop an activity to illustrate a specific principle of active learning, give it a summary of that principle and an example of its use. In fact, giving several examples can lead the AI to perform much

---

[18] Kojima, T., Gu, S. S., Reid, M., Matsuo, Y., & Iwasawa, Y. (2023, 29 January). Large Language Models are zero-shot reasoners. https://arxiv.org/abs/2205.11916

better.[19] However, as noted in the previous section, we must be cautious about sharing private or sensitive information with AIs.

- ***Specified factors and variables:*** Specify what factors or variables the AI should focus on, in both the input and the output. First, tell it what to focus on in the input. For example, if you want an AI to teach learners how to classify specific types of modern art, tell it to focus on the subject matter, brush technique, color pallets and any other factors that distinguish specific types. Second, specify the product or response you want. For example, if you want the AI to develop a particular type of game, give it details of what the game should be like; if you want it to develop an exercise for middle-school learners, include that information. In addition, set the AI to respond at a particular level of granularity, such as by providing ten examples, points, or responses.

In short, we can often avoid potential pitfalls of using AI to design, deliver, and assess active learning by creating appropriate prompts. We can also get very far by engaging AI in a systematic and principled way. In order to do so, we first need to consider the science behind active learning—which, at its core, relates to how the brain works. Thus, we turn to the science of learning in the following chapter. This chapter provides the foundations of the five principles of learning, which allow us to deploy AI systematically, effectively, and efficiently to help learners master new material.

---

[19] Mollick, E. (2023, 13 August), Automating creativity. https://www.oneusefulthing.org/p/automating-creativity?utm_source=substack&utm_medium=email

—3—

The Science of Learning

As you head to sleep each night, do you ever look back on the events of the day, reflecting on what you remember from the day gone by? When I've taught the science of learning, I've regularly asked this question. The vast majority of people confirm that they sometimes engage in this retrospective review. But this isn't really what I'm interested in. I follow this up with a second question: How much of what you recall about the events of your day do you think you *tried* to memorize as the event was taking place? I regularly meet a stunned, silent response.

"Raise your hand," I say, "if you *intentionally* memorized at least *half* of what you later recalled." After asking some two thousand thoughtful audience members, I've not seen a single hand go up.

I persist: "Have you intentionally memorized at least one-quarter of what you recalled that day?" Three people have raised their hands so far. I then ask the audience to raise their hands if they intentionally memorized about 20%, then 15%, and so on, reducing the amount in increments of 5%. The majority of people consistently raise their hands in the range of 5-10%.

Even if these self-reports are off by half, the responses are remarkable: Although we may assume that we remember what we have intentionally tried to learn, we typically do not try to memorize the vast majority of what we later recall. This raises a fundamental question: If we don't try to learn what happened during the day, how can we recall it later?

In fact, the science of learning aligns well with what I've been hearing in response to my questions. Most of what we recall results from what is known as *incidental learning*—it is simply a byproduct of paying attention and thinking about the event or material. As we discuss in the following chapter, most memory is actually a spin-off of mental processing—it's just something we pick up along the way.

This is only one of many findings from the science of learning, but it illustrates a key point: Much of what researchers have discovered about learning is not intuitively obvious. The situation reminds me of the old saying, "The fish is the last one to find out about water": We are so immersed in our daily lives that we take our mental processes for granted and rarely pause to consider their workings—even when they are accessible to our consciousness, which they often are not. [20] In this chapter, we briefly review the aspects of the science of learning that are most important for designing, delivering, and assessing active learning with AI.

Principles of the Science of Learning

The principles of the science of learning are the key to getting the most out of using AI for active learning. Rather than try to provide a long list of specific research findings, I have organized them into general principles: These principles allow you to deploy AI to design, deliver, and assess many types of active learning in a systematic, effective, and efficient way.

The principles in this book are practical:

- Each of them grows out of a large set of empirical findings,

---

[20] For example, see Damasio, A. (1994/2005). *Descartes's error: Emotion, reason, and the human brain*. New York: Penguin; Libet, B. (2005). *Mind time: The temporal factor in consciousness*. Cambridge, MA: Harvard University Press.

not isolated individual studies.[21]

- They capture highly replicable phenomena; they reflect regularities that appeared across many studies.

- The results from the relevant studies produced large effect sizes; the technique "moves the needle," it isn't simply "statistically significant."

- The principles are very general, applying to both knowledge and skills; using these principles can help in all sorts of learning.

However, although the principles distill results from "basic" research about how the brain works, they are augmented and fleshed out by studies that identify specific interventions that improve learning. For example, the anecdote about incidental learning illustrates the Principle of Deep Processing, which states that "*The more mental processing one performs on information, the more likely it is that one will retain that information.*"[22] Researchers fleshed out this principle in many ways. For instance, they showed that the mere act of taking a test, which leads one to think deeply about the material, helps people to learn—even if learners are not told the correct answers afterward.[23]

The science of learning is broader than it might seem at first glance. "Learning" and "memory" are treated as different sides of the same coin: Memory is the result of learning; without memory, learning may as well not have occurred. And without learning, there can be no memory. Moreover, learning is not just about acquiring new knowledge or skills. Yes, some learning is simple memorization (e.g., of vocabulary words in a new language), but most learning is more than that: Learning requires that you comprehend the material, which means that you need to relate it to other

---

[21] When citing a line of work, I often cite the "classic" study that had the initial insight; the fact that these studies have stood the test of time is important.

[22] By "information," I mean data that has been interpreted so that it has meaning (e.g., as a fact, concept, word, image, or procedure).

[23] Roediger, H. L., & Karpicke, J. D. (2006). Test-enhanced learning: Taking memory tests improves long-term retention. *Psychological Science, 17*, 249–255.

things you already know. And learning requires that you know how to apply the information in relevant contexts, "transferring" it appropriately, not simply leave it in cold storage.

In this book, when I talk about learning specific material, what I mean is that learners will come to comprehend, retain and know how to apply that material appropriately.

The science of learning has three main branches:

- The first addresses how we organize and interpret information in a way that will lodge it in our brain's memory banks. To learn something, we need to make it coherent, which requires organizing and interpreting it appropriately.
- The second branch addresses how we actually store and retain information.
- The third branch addresses how we access and apply the stored information when it is relevant. If we cannot retrieve or use stored information, it may as well not exist.

In what follows, I consider only the aspects of the science of learning that provide the foundations for the principles I have abstracted from the literature.[24] We will build on these foundations in the following chapters as we consider how to use these principles to guide active learning with AI.

Organizing and Interpreting

The first step to learning is to organize the relevant information. Our brains rely on two kinds of processes to do so. First, *bottom-up* processes are governed by the physical characteristics of objects and events in the world. For example, imagine that you grew up in a small, rural country and have left it for the very first time to visit a large, bustling American city. You are taking a walk in a beautiful, sprawling park, and you take a turn on the path and suddenly see a merry-go-round. You have never seen such a

---

[24] If you want more detail, see Gazzaniga, M., Ivry, R. B., & Mangun, G. R. (2018). *Cognitive neuroscience: The biology of the mind* (5th ed). New York: W. W. Norton; or, Smith, E.E., & Kosslyn, S. M. (2006). *Cognitive psychology: Mind and brain*. New York, NY: Prentice Hall.

thing before and have no idea what it is. This could be overwhelming. However, after even a few seconds of seeing this, your brain has already begun to organize the scene. You notice that different objects are painted different colors and are moving up and down differently, which leads you to see them as distinct. You notice their body shapes and the fact that small people are riding on their upper surfaces, which leads you to see them as horses. However, you also notice that they are rigid and would soon conclude that they are made of wood or a similar material. You also notice that they are on poles attached to the floor and ceiling and that the entire herd of wooden animals is moving together around the center of a round, rotating room. These various physical characteristics allow you to organize this massive amount of information.

The sorts of physical characteristics that govern bottom-up processing often result in our organizing things hierarchically. Going back to the merry-go-round, you soon would see that the entire ensemble is a single construction, a rotating room populated by wooden horses. You might begin to see clusters of these horses based on how they are arranged. And in each cluster, you would see that each individual horse has a head, legs, a tail, a place for a rider to sit, and so on. You would break down the entire scene into groups of objects, and each object into a set of smaller objects, including parts. This is the essence of hierarchical organization. In Chapter 5, on chunking, we will explore in more detail specific rules that govern how we use bottom-up processing to organize what we perceive.

As schematized in Figure 3.1, we humans also organize information by using *top-down processing,* which is governed by our knowledge, beliefs, and goals. For example, consider what happens when you return to the park the following day, and come around that bend in the path and see the merry-go-round. This will be a very different experience than it was the first day. Why? Because your brain will now be using what you learned the previous day to make sense of what you are seeing and hearing. The knowledge you stored will guide you to organize the scene. However, such top-down processing is a two-edged sword: It is efficient and fast, but it also may run roughshod over what's actually out there. For example, I recall one time I was searching for a friend's handbag and thought I had found it in the corner of her bedroom. Reaching down to pick it up, I was startled when her black cat squirmed out of my reach. I was expecting to see her handbag, and when I saw something the right color and size, I inappropriately imposed my expectation, top-down, on what was actually there.

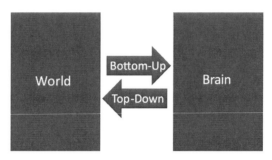

Figure 3.1. Top-down versus bottom-up processing.

Once we have organized information, typically using a combination of bottom-up and top-down processing, we need to make sense of it. This requires comparing what we currently are perceiving with information we have previously stored in our brain's memory banks. To take a very simple example, say that you see a red, slightly lumpy round thing that's about four inches in diameter. Relying on bottom-up processing, your brain may match it to several objects you've seen before and stored information about: an apple, a tomato, and a small felt ball. To distinguish among them, you would then take a second look. You would now be guided by top-down processing to look for features that would distinguish among the possibilities, such as a certain sized and shaped stem at the top. Finding one, you would know that it's an apple.

This same process, where knowledge stored in your brain is applied to the current situation, allows us to make sense not just of the physical world but also of language, social cues, and everything else. For example, this is how you know what a smile or frown means. It all begins with organizing what we perceive and then using what we've learned previously to interpret it.

Storing Information

Once we have organized and interpreted information, we are poised to store that information in our brain's memory banks.

One fundamental discovery from cognitive psychology is that our brains have more than one type of memory bank.[25] We usually begin to learn something by first storing it in *short-term memory,* which is sometimes called *working memory.*[26] When information is in short-term memory, we are consciously aware of it. For example, when you are sent a code for two-factor verification, you store it in short-term memory between the moment of seeing it on your screen and when you finish tapping in the numbers. This example illustrates two crucial facts about short-term memory: First, we can retain information in short-term memory only very briefly, which can be frustrating if you get the verification code on one device and need to enter it into another. We can retain the information for about half a minute by repeating it over and over, with a lot of effort. Second, we can hold only three or four groups in short-term memory. To retain the verification code, you need to organize it quickly (e.g., into two groups of three digits). Short-term memory plays a key role when we organize information as the initial step to learning it. Hence, the fact that short-term memory has only a very small capacity is important during learning.

Clearly, I would not be happy if you, dear reader, only stored information about the science of learning in your short-term memory. I hope that you will store that information in your *long-term memory,* which contains everything you have learned and retained over your lifetime—all

---

[25] For an expanded treatment, see Kosslyn, S. M., & Rosenberg, R. S. (2020). *Introducing psychology: Brain, person, group (5th edition).* Boston, MA: FlatWorld

[26] The concept of Working Memory is sometimes treated as a more modern version of the concept of Short-Term Memory, but it is in fact a broader concept—including processes that operate on what is in memory in addition to the memory store itself. I focus here on the memory store per se; cf. Baddeley, A.D. (2007). *Working memory, thought and action.* Oxford: Oxford University Press; Baddeley, A.D. (2010). Working memory. *Current Biology, 20,* R136-R140.

the facts, words, concepts, images, rules, procedures, and so on. One goal of teaching is to help learners convert what's in their short-term memories to material they store in their long-term memories. We aim to devise ways to help learners store information in a durable form, so they can later recall and use this information.

The brain stores information in long-term memory in multiple ways. As we discuss in Chapter 7, learning is enhanced when people store both words and images. This results in part because every perceptual system (e.g., vision, hearing, touch) also stores "modality specific" memories, both short-term and long-term. For example, we have visual long-term memories, which we can recall to produce visual mental images in short-term memory. For instance, please answer this question: What shape are Mickey Mouse's ears? In order to answer, most people visualize the cartoon character and "look" at the ears in their mental image to "see" that they are circular. The visual information was present in long-term memory, but to access it, you needed to bring it into short-term memory and hence become conscious of it.[27]

However, when we hear or read a description, such as a fact about the science of learning, we typically do not store the words, phrases, or sentences themselves; rather, we store the concepts that are conveyed by language—we store the meaning, the *gist*, not the specific words. People who speak more than one language may even forget which language was used to describe something. They store the meaning, not the words themselves. This type of memory differs from the modality-specific perceptual memory of the words as we hear them, which specifies how they sound when spoken by a particular person, or as we read them, which specifies how they look when printed in a particular font. Most

---

[27] For more about mental imagery, see Kosslyn, S. M. (1980). *Image and mind.* Cambridge, MA: Harvard University Press; Kosslyn, S.M. (1994). *Image and brain.* Cambridge, MA: MIT Press; Pearson, J., Naselaris, T., Holmes, E.A., & Kosslyn, S.M. (2015). Mental imagery: Functional mechanisms and clinical applications. *Trends in Cognitive Science, 19,* 590-602. doi: 10.1016/j.tics.2015.08.003. PMID: 26412097; PMCID: PMC4595480; Sulfaro, A., Robinson, A. K., & Carlson, T. A. (2023). Comparing mental imagery experiences across visual, auditory, and other sensory modalities. biRxiv preprint : https://doi.org/10.1101/2023.05.15.540306;

"academic" knowledge is of this "gist" type, which draws deeply on language, be it heard (in lectures, in discussions) or read (in textbooks, in documents).

Did you know that there's a type of knowledge that you can't call into consciousness? For instance, do you know how you are able to keep your balance on a bike? All of what we have discussed so far focuses on information that we can bring into short-term memory, as in the Mickey Mouse example, but a lot of what we know we can only access when we are actually using it. The first sort of knowledge is often called *declarative* knowledge and includes facts, concepts, words, and images. The second sort of information is often called *procedural* knowledge and includes skills such as your knowledge of how to do arithmetic, ride a bike, or produce grammatical sentences in your native language.

Procedural memories enable us to perform tasks "automatically" without needing to consciously think about what we are doing.[28] We often begin by learning declarative information about a rule or process, but after we use it a lot, it becomes a procedural memory and hence automatic. For example, when first learning a new language, you are probably very aware of the specific rules of grammar, but with practice, you can form sentences automatically and intuitively. Or when you are first learning to drive a car, you consciously think through every step, but with practice, the knowledge becomes procedural and automatic.

For present purposes, the main reason to keep in mind the distinction between declarative and procedural knowledge concerns our limited short-term memory capacity: This is a major bottleneck in how well we can draw on declarative information when we learn and reason, but does not affect how well we can draw on procedural information. When you can perform a skill automatically, you remove the burden on short-term

---

[28] Anderson, J. R., Bothell, D., Byrne, M. D., Douglass, S., Lebiere, C., & Qin, Y. (2004). An integrated theory of the mind. *Psychological Review, 111*, 1036-1060; Clark, R. E. (2011). The impact of non-conscious knowledge on educational technology research and design. *Educational Technology, July-August,* 3-11; Squire, L.R. (2004). Memory systems of the brain: A brief history and current perspective. *Neurobiology of Learning and Memory, 82*, 171–177.

memory—freeing it up to do other things.[29] For instance, after you have a lot of practice driving a car, you have no problem carrying on a conversation while steering, braking, watching out for obstacles, and so forth. But having a conversation with a beginner while they're driving is an invitation to disaster—they need to rely on that short-term memory capacity to drive, and shouldn't be distracted.

As summarized in Figure 3.2. there is clearly more than one way to learn and remember. As we shall see in Chapter 7, the Principle of Dual Coding capitalizes on this fact by leading instructors and course designers to help learners absorb the material in at least two different ways, typically verbally and visually.[30]

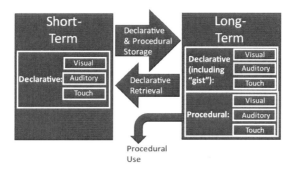

Figure 3.2. Types of memories. We are consciously aware only of what is in Short-Term Memory. We cannot voluntarily bring procedural memories into Short-Term Memory. Long-Term Memory includes both declarative and procedural modality-specific memories (such as visual, auditory, and touch, which are common examples of modality-specific memories) as well as "gist" declarative memories.

---

[29] Sweller, J., Ayres, J., & Kalyuga, S. (2011). *Cognitive load theory*. New York: Springer-Verlag.

[30] However, I must note that in spite of this fact, there is no evidence that some of us are "visual learners," others "verbal learners," and so forth—we all can use the different modalities effectively. See Pashler, H., McDaniel, M., Rohrer, D., & Bjork, R. (2008). Learning styles: Concepts and evidence. *Psychological Science in the Public Interest, 9*, 105-119; Willingham, D. T. (2009). *Why don't students like school? A cognitive scientist answers questions about how the mind works and what it means for the classroom*. San Francisco, CA: Wiley/Jossey-Bass

Accessing Stored Information

Memories are only useful if you can access them. Managing to sock away in memory the concepts of the science of learning, for example, won't do you any good if you cannot later access this information when designing courses, delivering them, and assessing them. By analogy, having the world's largest collection of digitized music would be useless if you didn't have a way to reach those files and send them to a device that plays them. Procedural and declarative memories are accessed in different ways. Procedural memories are accessed by the appropriate "trigger" conditions. You access your knowledge of how to drive when you are behind the wheel of a car; you employ the rules of grammar when you are listening to and speaking a language. In contrast, declarative memories are accessed using internal or external cues, and this is what we will focus on because most formal learning is about acquiring declarative information (e.g., facts, concepts, rules, and images).

Declarative memories aren't stored like neatly alphabetized files in a filing cabinet. Rather, they are cross-referenced directly and indirectly via other stored information. We don't just recall that birds have feathers; we also know that they are animals, and hence eat and breathe, that they have a distant relationship to dinosaurs, and perhaps that they have hollow bones, which is useful for flying. Everything we know fits into a web of knowledge and belief that we store in long-term memory. As we shall see in Chapter 6, when we consider the Principle of Associations, such a rich set of associations plays a crucial role in how we can rely on top-down processing to organize new information in order to enter it into long-term memory, how we retain information securely in long-term memory over time, and how we later access that information when we want to apply it. In particular, associated information can serve as *retrieval cues*, hints that jog our memories and allow us to recall specific information. For example, if you study a set of facts while listening to an album you just got, that music later will probably serve to remind you of those facts.

Assessing Learning

We sometimes want learners to access stored information in order to demonstrate that they did, in fact, successfully learn the material. Figuring out how much learning has taken place requires devising ways to have learners demonstrate their knowledge. As we shall see in subsequent chapters, AI can help us do this. All forms of assessments fall into one of the following three categories.

First, you can ask learners to *recall* the information, which requires them to dig it out of long-term memory and activate it in short-term memory so that they are aware of it—which in turn allows them to use it in various ways. For example, asking learners to summarize material, such as the principles of the science of learning, requires them to recall that information—as does asking them to describe key facts about a Civil War battle or to explain how an AI works.

Second, rather than asking learners to recall information, you can ask them to *recognize* it. In this case, you would ask them to pick out the correct alternative from a set of choices or to decide whether an assertion is correct. To recognize the correct answer, learners need to match the choices or assertion to what they previously stored in long-term memory. This process relies on the same brain mechanisms that allow us to interpret and make sense of things we encounter as we navigate the world, as discussed earlier. But in this situation, we are looking for cases where the process succeeds versus breaks down: If learners don't store the information effectively, and hence don't really "know" the material, they will have trouble later recognizing it. Multiple-choice and True/False tests are the classic ways to draw on recognition to assess what learners know.

Third, often drawing on procedural knowledge, you can assess skills by asking learners to *demonstrate* them. If you want to know whether someone learned to draw using perspective, to pronounce words correctly in Arabic, to employ a 7-iron in golf appropriately, or to use rhetorical techniques to deliver a powerful speech, have them actually demonstrate the relevant behavior. The three means of assessment are schematized in Figure 3.3.

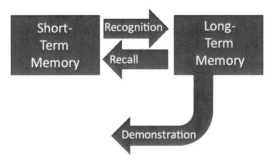

Figure 3.3. Recall versus Recognition versus Demonstration.

The differences among recognition, recall, and demonstration are important in part because we can use recognition to give us feedback even when we cannot recall or utilize the stored information perfectly—which can help us to learn new things. For example, when learning to play a new piece of music, you might not recall all of it and randomly begin to play different notes until you hit on a sequence that you recognize. This will, in turn, help you learn the piece. This use of recognition is critical for the Principle of Deliberate Practice, which we consider in Chapter 8.

Transfer

Finally, people tend not to deploy information outside of the narrow context where they learned it. This is a problem because the goal of teaching is not simply to help learners score highly on tests and course assignments. Rather, we want learners to use what they learn in class when they later make decisions, solve problems, or create something new at work and in their daily lives. Achieving this goal requires learners to transfer what they learn from one context to another.

Consider this anecdote a colleague told me: His friend was asked to teach an undergraduate physics course to learners who were majoring in other fields. To make the course interesting, he decided to provide a lot of examples from baseball. A lot of physics is evident in baseball—for example, Newton's Third Law is at work when a bat hits a ball. The problem was that he drew on so many baseball examples in his lectures that he ran out of them by the time of the final exam. So, instead, he used football examples for the final exam. The result? The class rebelled! The common sentiment ran along the lines of "The whole course was about baseball, and then you tricked us in the final, switching to football! This isn't fair!!" (I'm not making this up.) This was a clear example of a failure of transfer, but in this case, this is a failure of *near transfer*—the original situation was similar to the new one, and they weren't separated much in time. In contrast, *far transfer* involves transferring knowledge or skills from one situation to another that seems dissimilar, and the situations are separated in time.[31] For example, far transfer occurs when you apply what you learned last year about tropical storms to what you are learning now about ant colonies, both of which are "complex systems."

To teach effectively, the methods of instruction should be designed to encourage both sorts of transfer, near and far. Nobody—not instructors, learners, parents or administrators—wants to teach material that stays in the classroom and is never drawn on by the learners outside of class.

My takeaway from the scientific literature is that we can encourage transfer largely via three practices:

- ***Combine examples and principles:*** Instructors and course designers should give learners a wide range of concrete examples and should explain in detail how they are related. Neither examples alone nor an underlying principle alone is sufficient. Learners need both examples and clear principles that tie them together. The goal is to help learners later easily bring to mind phrases such as "It reminds me of...", "It's like...", and "It's the same as..." when they encounter related

---

[31] Barnett, S., & Ceci, S. (2002). When and where do we apply what we learn? A taxonomy for far transfer. *Psychological Bulletin 128*, 612-637. For evidence that far transfer is difficult to achieve, see Gobet, F., & Sala, Giovanni. (2022). Cognitive training: A field in search of a phenomenon. *Perspectives on Psychological Science, 18*, https://doi.org/10.1177/17456916221091830

situations or material.[32]

- **Create learning objectives for the use case:** Instructors and course designers should help learners achieve learning outcomes that correspond as closely as possible to what learners actually want to do at work or in their daily lives. This goal requires specific, concrete, and measurable learning objectives that are also directly relevant. For example, if the instructor wants to teach learners to become critical consumers of news, one learning objective should lead learners to evaluate whether a news source is probably biased.

- **Create activities similar to the use case:** Instructors or course designers should design activities that are as close as possible to what learners will actually do outside of class. For example, if the goal is to teach negotiation skills, a role-playing activity that mimics actual negotiations is better than a problem-solving activity where learners try to determine the best approach.

This brief overview provides the foundations of the principles we shall encounter in the following six chapters. We next consider what many regard as the single most important principle in the science of learning, the Principle of Deep Processing, and see in detail how to use AI to leverage this principle to help learners acquire new knowledge and skills.

---

[32] Haskell, R. E. (2000). *Transfer of learning: Cognition, instruction, and reasoning.* New York: Academic Press; Kober, N. (2015). *Reaching students: What research says about effective instruction in undergraduate science and engineering.* Board on Science Education, Division of Behavioral and Social Sciences and Education. Washington, DC: The National Academies Press.

—4—

Deep Processing

My favorite experiment in all of cognitive psychology was reported by Gordon H. Bower in 1970.[33] Here's what he did: He asked participants to listen to a lengthy list of pairs of words, such as "cow-tree," "fork-guitar," and "bag-rock." The participants were organized into three groups, which received the same list of pairs of words but had different instructions about what to do with them. One group was asked to say the pairs of words silently to themselves, over and over, and to try to memorize which words went together. A second group was asked to visualize the named objects interacting in some way (e.g., a cow rubbing against a tree, a guitar with a fork stuck into it) and to memorize which words went together. And a third group was asked simply to visualize the named objects interacting in some way and then to rate how vivid the mental image was, ranging from very dim and vague to very sharp and realistic. This last group was not told anything about trying to memorize the pairs of words and was not warned of an impending memory test.

After going through all of the pairs of words, the investigator gave all three groups a memory test where they got the first word of each pair (e.g.,

---

[33] Bower, G. H. (1972). Mental imagery and associative learning. In L. Gregg (Ed.), *Cognition in learning and memory* (pp. 51-88). New York: John Wiley & Sons.

"cow," "fork," and "bag") and were supposed to recall the other word in that pair. The results were straightforward: The second group, which visualized the objects interacting and tried to memorize them, recalled about twice as much as the first group, which silently verbalized the names and tried to memorize them. And the third group—which visualized the objects interacting but did not try to memorize them—did as well as the second group and did about twice as well as the group that verbalized the names and tried to memorize them.

This last finding is remarkable: The mere act of creating the mental images and "looking at them" with the mind's eye to rate their vividness was enough to lodge the associations in memory—even though the participants were not trying to memorize the word pairs. This is very much along the lines of the sorts of memories you have of events that took place earlier in the day, the vast majority of which you did not try to memorize at the time they occurred.

These kinds of phenomena illustrate the Principle of Deep Processing, which states that "*The more mental processing one performs on information, the more likely it is that one will retain that information.*"[34]

The Principle of Deep Processing lies at the core of why active learning works; it is the central principle that underlies why active learning is better than passive learning, such as occurs when learners sit and listen to a lecture. The other principles either set the stage for engaging in specific types of deep processing or augment this principle in some way.

I have often demonstrated this principle to large groups. Pretend that you are an audience participant, and get a sense of what it's like to do these tasks.

---

[34] For a different treatment of this principle, see Kosslyn, S.M. (2017). The science of learning. In S. M. Kosslyn & B. Nelson. (Eds.), *Building the intentional university*. Cambridge, MA: MIT Press. See also Craik, F. I. M., & Lockhart, R. S. (1972). Levels of processing: A framework for memory research. *Journal of Verbal Learning and Verbal Behavior, 11,* 671-684; Craig, S. D., Sullins, J., Witherspoon, A., & Gholson, B. (2006). The deep-level reasoning effect: The role of dialogue and deep-level-reasoning questions during vicarious learning. *Cognition and Instruction, 24,* 565-591.

1. I tell you, the audience, that you will soon see a list of words and I will ask you to do one of two things with each word.

2. If you see "Living?" in front of a word, silently decide whether or not that word names a living thing (e.g., "tree" does, "rock" does not).

3. If you see "Height?" in front of a word, silently decide whether the first letter of the word ascends higher than the letter at the end of the word (e.g., in this font, the "h" in "house" ascends higher than the "e," but the "m" in "most" does not ascend higher than the "t" and the "s" in "seam" does not ascend higher than the "m.").

4. I then give you, the audience, a short practice list to ensure that everyone understands the instructions:

(Living?)	lizard
(Height?)	ant
(Height?)	dog
(Living?)	brick

5. I ask you to evaluate each word in this practice list aloud (and the answers are Yes, No, Yes, No).

6. Following this, I show you the following list and ask you to go through it, silently classifying each word as indicated, not writing anything down (try this yourself). I ask the audience to raise their hands when they are finished and I wait until virtually every hand is raised.

(Living?)	frog
(Height?)	rat
(Height?)	sheet
(Living?)	bread
(Height?)	deer
(Living?)	rug
(Height?)	forge

(Living?)	bear
(Height?)	hare
(Height?)	lamp
(Living?)	stone
(Height?)	chair
(Living?)	ape
(Height?)	worm
(Living?)	snail
(Living?)	harp

7. I remove the list, and 5-10 seconds later, without prior warning, I ask you to recall as many words that were on the list as possible. (This is often met with groans.) I tell you, the audience, that you have 20 seconds to write down the words or just bring them to mind.

8. Following this, I show two lists, one for the words judged as living/nonliving and one for the words judged in terms of letter height. I ask the audience to count how many words they correctly recalled in each list. (And I tell everyone that they are on the Honor System!)

9. And finally, I ask the audience members to compare the number they got right following each judgment—and to respond to a poll to indicate which judgment led to better memory.

The typical result: The vast majority of people recall more words following the living/nonliving judgment than the height judgment. Why? Judging whether a word names a living thing requires more mental processing than judging surface properties like height. To decide whether a named object is living, a participant needs to dig into their memory and think about characteristics of the object, such as whether it moves of its own volition or is a plant. But to decide which letter is higher, they just need to look at what they were given, with no need to dig into memory.

In short: The more a person processes information mentally, the more likely they are to recall it later—even if they weren't trying to learn it.

Targeted Processing

To use the Principle of Deep Processing in active learning with AI, it's crucial to ensure that the activity guides the learners to process deeply the information that underlies the learning objective. For example, consider the implications of one classic study:[35] Participants began by seeing a list of words, and half of them judged an aspect of each word's meaning and half judged whether each word rhymes with another particular word. Following this, the investigators gave the participants a memory test, and led half of the people in each of the two groups to focus on the meanings of the words and half to focus on the sounds of the words.

The important finding: Participants who initially judged the meanings of words later recalled the words better when focusing on their meanings than when focusing on how they sounded. But exactly the opposite was found when participants initially judged how words sounded. In this case, they later were better at remembering words with specific sounds than words that had specific meanings.

The point is that more mental processing results in better memory *of what was processed*. It's not that one sort of judgment or type of processing always leads to better learning, and it's not the sheer amount of mental processing that's important. Rather, what is important is the amount of processing of the relevant information. In the vast majority of cases, focusing on meaning is crucial because you will later want to rely on the meaning when you use that information. Thus, the goal is to focus the learners on the relevant aspects of the meaning of the material.

The fact that learners remember what they focus on and process deeply applies to more than memorizing words. It applies in general to

---

[35] Morris, D. C., Bransford, J. D., & Franks, J. J. (1977). Levels of processing versus transfer appropriate processing. *Journal of Verbal Learning and Verbal Behavior, 16,* 519-533.

learning all knowledge and skills.[36] You get what you teach. This fact underscores the importance of having clear learning objectives from the outset. As I stressed earlier, the crucial first step to designing active learning is to define the learning objectives. Your learning objectives govern what you want the learners to focus on during active learning. An AI can help. For example, see Box 2.

BOX 2: Using AI to create a sequence of learning objectives

Me:
Can you put together a sequence of learning objectives that can be used to help students master the concept of supply and demand?

AI:
Certainly! Here's a sequence of learning objectives to help students master the concept of supply and demand:

1. Define key terms and concepts in the context of supply and demand, such as quantity supplied, quantity demanded, equilibrium, and market-clearing price.
2. Explain the laws of supply and demand, demonstrating an understanding of how price affects the quantity supplied and demanded.
3. Identify factors that can influence supply and demand, such as production costs, consumer preferences, income levels, and prices of related goods (substitutes and complements).
4. Graph supply and demand curves, demonstrating an understanding of the relationship between price and quantity on each curve.
5. Determine the market equilibrium point on a supply and demand graph, identifying the equilibrium price and quantity.

---

[36] Berry, J.W., & Chew, S.L., (2008). Improving learning through interventions of student-generated questions and concept maps. *Teaching of Psychology, 35*, 305-312; Chew, S.L. (2005). Seldom in doubt but often wrong: Addressing tenacious student misconceptions. In D.S. Dunn, & S.L. Chew, (Eds.), *Best practices in teaching general psychology* (pp. 211-223). Mahwah, NJ: Erlbaum; Nolen, S. B. (1988). Reasons for studying: Motivational orientations and study strategies. *Cognition and Instruction, 5*, 269-287.

6. Analyze the effects of changes in supply and demand factors on market equilibrium, predicting shifts in the supply and demand curves and the resulting changes in equilibrium price and quantity.
7. Apply the concept of supply and demand to real-world scenarios, evaluating the impact of economic events on markets and explaining price changes using the principles of supply and demand.
8. Evaluate the efficiency of resource allocation in a market based on supply and demand principles, recognizing the role of market forces in achieving an efficient allocation of resources.

By following this sequence of learning objectives, students will gain a thorough understanding of the concept of supply and demand and its application to various economic situations.

Once you are armed with appropriate learning objectives, you can structure an activity to lead learners to process the relevant information deeply. For example, say that the learning objective is to employ eight negotiation tactics effectively. We can help learners achieve this learning objective by asking them to participate in a simulated negotiation role-playing game, with an AI playing some of the roles. Consider the following instructions to the learners and prompt to the AI, the results from which are presented in Box 3.

Instructions to the Learner

You are going to play a role in a negotiation with an AI. The point of this exercise is for you to see how to use eight negotiation tactics effectively. To master this learning objective you will negotiate how a school district selects new computers. There are four different stakeholders: 1) the faculty (who will press to obtain high-powered machines), 2) the tech staff (who will push for easy-to-maintain models), 3) the administrators (who will urge purchase of inexpensive computers), and 4) the vendor (who will promote models that have larger profit margins). Each of these roles will use a different pair of negotiating tactics. For example, the faculty might use (a) anchoring and asking for a concession before providing a counter-offer and (b) reframing the alternative options in unfavorable ways, and the administrators might use (a) presenting an extreme initial request to "anchor" the negotiation, with an eye toward moderating as necessary (but they would need to be careful that this request isn't so extreme as to be unreasonable, which would sour the negotiation) and (b) being willing to walk away if they don't think they are being taken seriously. The AI will assign you one of the roles at random and will tell you which two negotiating tactics to use. You should not only stick to your two tactics, but also should try to infer the negotiation tactics being used by each of the other roles—and should be prepared to evaluate how well they used those tactics and to justify your evaluations. At the end of the exercise, you will be asked to turn into the instructor your evaluations of how effectively the other stakeholders each used their tactics and why you made these evaluations. When you are ready to begin, paste the following prompt into your AI input window, and take it from there!

AI Prompt

You are going to conduct a role-playing simulation of a negotiation with a human student. The learning objective is: "Use eight negotiation tactics effectively." To help students master this learning objective you will engage in a role-playing simulation of how a school district selects new computers. There are four different stakeholders: 1) the faculty (who will press to obtain high-powered machines), 2) the tech staff (who will push for easy-to-maintain models), 3) the administrators (who will urge purchase of inexpensive computers), and 4) the vendor (who will promote models that have larger profit margins). You will assign two different negotiating tactics to each role. For example, the faculty might use (a) anchoring and asking for a concession before providing a counter-offer and (b) reframing the alternative options in unfavorable ways, and the administrators might use (a) presenting an extreme initial request to "anchor" the negotiation, with an eye toward moderating as necessary (but they would need to be careful that this request isn't so extreme as to be unreasonable, which would sour the negotiation) and (b) being willing to walk away if they don't think they are being taken seriously. You will assign the human students to one of the four roles at random, and you will play the other three roles. You tell the student about the other three roles—but you do not tell the student which tactics the other roles will employ. Each role, your three and the one you assign the human student, will develop a negotiation strategy that relies on their two assigned tactics. Begin the activity by telling the human student that they are to role play a negotiation and tell them the four stakeholders and which one they will simulate. Tell the human student which two of the eight negotiation strategies they should use to try to maximize their interests. Then begin by having one of your roles make an initial proposal. When the student responds, have another one of your roles then respond. Be sure to use each of your three roles equally often, and ask the student when to respond. Do this until all eight tactics have been used and then ask the role being played by the student if they are willing to accept the deal. If so, end the negotiation; if not repeat for another round and ask again. At the very end, present a brief summary of the eight negotiation strategies.

BOX 3: Using AI to conduct a role-playing simulation

AI:
Welcome to the role-playing negotiation simulation! In this activity, you'll be representing one of the four stakeholders involved in selecting new computers for a school district. The stakeholders are:

1. Faculty
2. Tech staff
3. Administrators
4. Vendor

You have been randomly assigned to the role of the tech staff. Your goal is to push for easy-to-maintain computer models. To help you achieve this objective, you should use the following two negotiation strategies:

1. Building rapport and finding common ground with other stakeholders.
2. Employing a "trade-off" strategy by making concessions in areas that are less important to you in exchange for gains in areas that matter more.

As for me, I will be playing the roles of the faculty, administrators, and the vendor. I will not disclose the negotiation tactics I'll be using for these roles.

Let's begin the negotiation.

AI: Faculty role:[37]
"We propose that the school should invest in high-powered computers with cutting-edge technology to enhance the students' learning experience. We think it's essential to have machines that can handle demanding applications, so our students are well-prepared for their future careers."

Now it's your turn to respond as the tech staff. Remember to use your negotiation tactics effectively.

Me:
I'm sure we all want what's best for all of the computer users at our school. Nobody likes to wait when their computers are broken. Thus, we should prioritize getting machines that are easy to maintain.

AI: Administrator role:
"While we understand the importance of having high-powered computers and easy maintenance, we must also consider our budget constraints. We propose selecting a cost-effective model that meets the basic requirements for our students and staff. It may not be the most powerful or the easiest to maintain, but it will be affordable, which is crucial for our school's financial health."

AI: Vendor role:
"We have a range of models that could fit the school's needs. Some are more powerful, while others focus on ease of maintenance or affordability. We could offer a discount if the school decides to purchase a larger quantity of computers. This way, we can find a balance between performance, maintenance, and cost."

---

[37] To remove any confusion, I've edited these headings to make it clear which role the AI is playing.

As the tech staff, feel free to respond and continue the negotiation. Remember to use your negotiation strategies effectively.

Me:
I'm willing to go for machines that are slightly less easy to maintain if the price is right and they are very powerful.

AI: Faculty role:
"We appreciate your flexibility, tech staff. It's important that we provide our students with powerful computers while also considering maintenance and cost. If we can find a model that strikes a good balance, it could be a win-win for everyone."

AI: Administrator role:
"That sounds like a reasonable compromise. We should look into the discounted options provided by the vendor and evaluate the trade-offs between power, maintenance, and cost. If we can find a solution that satisfies all parties, we can move forward with the purchase."

Now, as the tech staff, feel free to respond and indicate if you are willing to accept the deal. If not, you may continue negotiating.

Me:
I'm happy with this deal.

AI:
Great! It looks like we've reached an agreement that takes into account the interests of all parties: powerful computers for the faculty, easy-to-maintain models for the tech staff, and cost-effective solutions for the administrators. The vendor's offer to provide a discount for a larger purchase has also contributed to achieving a satisfactory outcome.

To summarize the negotiation tactics used in this simulation:

1. Faculty: a) Anchoring and asking for a concession before providing a counter-offer, b) Reframing the alternative options in unfavorable ways.
2. Tech staff (your role): a) Building rapport and finding common ground with other stakeholders, b) Employing a "trade-off" strategy

by making concessions in areas that are less important in exchange for gains in areas that matter more.
3. Administrators: a) Presenting an extreme initial request to "anchor" the negotiation, with an eye toward moderating as necessary, b) Being willing to walk away if they don't think they are being taken seriously.
4. Vendor: a) Offering incentives (discounts) to encourage a deal, b) Demonstrating flexibility by presenting a range of models that cater to the varying needs of the stakeholders.

Congratulations on successfully completing the negotiation simulation!

The AI's responses aren't perfect, for example the faculty role didn't really seem to draw on the anchoring technique. But that can actually be an advantage here: The main task for the learners is to evaluate how effectively each role deployed their tactics and to justify those evaluations. Thus, we can turn a sow's ear into a silk purse: the deficits in negotiation can encourage the learners to engage in deep processing during their evaluations.

Another technique to induce targeted deep processing is a "Jigsaw activity."[38] In this case, you start with sets of groups that each address a different aspect of a task. [39] After each of those groups meets and discusses its distinct role, you then break up those groups and create new ones that have one member from each of the initial groups. Box 4 presents an example that an AI produced when I asked it how to teach the

---

[38] See: https://en.wikipedia.org/wiki/Jigsaw_learning_technique; https://en.wikipedia.org/wiki/ Jigsaw_(teaching_technique)

[39] Most of this book is written from the perspective of hybrid classes that use a Learning Management System to deliver content and an AI to provide live, interactive active learning. However, some courses will have synchronous sections, in person or via an online platform, such as Engageli or Zoom. Thus, I've provided a few examples of how AI can produce group activities, which also can be carried out via a discussion thread in asynchronous sessions. However, if individual learners do not interact in your course, it is easy to modify the prompt so that the AI plays the roles of other learners (just as it played the roles of different stakeholders in Box 3).

differences between prokaryotic and eukaryotic gene expression. This is an example of an active learning exercise that is designed to be delivered off line, at a later time, perhaps via a Learning Management System.

BOX 4: Using AI to create and conduct a Jigsaw activity

AI:
A good active learning exercise to teach the differences between prokaryotic and eukaryotic gene expression could be a "Jigsaw Activity." This approach involves dividing the class into small groups, with each group responsible for learning and teaching a specific aspect of the topic. Here's a step-by-step guide to implementing this exercise:

1. Divide the class into four "expert" groups, with each group focusing on one of the following aspects of prokaryotic and eukaryotic gene expression:
   a. Organization of genetic material
   b. Transcription and translation
   c. RNA processing
   d. Regulation of gene expression
2. Provide each expert group with resources and materials relevant to their assigned aspect. Encourage them to read, discuss, and summarize the key differences between prokaryotic and eukaryotic gene expression for their specific aspect.
3. Once the expert groups have become knowledgeable about their assigned aspect, reorganize the class into new "jigsaw" groups. Each jigsaw group should have one representative from each expert group, ensuring that all four aspects are covered within each jigsaw group.
4. In their jigsaw groups, students take turns teaching their peers about the key differences between prokaryotic and eukaryotic gene expression for their assigned aspect. Encourage active discussion, questions, and clarification.
5. After the jigsaw activity is completed, bring the class together for a whole-class discussion. Review and summarize the key differences between prokaryotic and eukaryotic gene expression, addressing any misconceptions or confusion that may have arisen during the activity.

6. Optionally, you may assign a follow-up assessment or activity to reinforce and assess students' understanding of the topic, such as creating a comparison chart or a concept map, or answering a set of questions that require them to apply their understanding of the differences between prokaryotic and eukaryotic gene expression.

Debates, role-playing, and jigsaw activities can easily be designed to lead the learners to focus on the material underlying a particular learning objective. Such activities require learners to process the relevant information deeply and hence they are likely to learn it. And more than that, these sorts of exercises can give them experience in using the key information in ways that should transfer to the relevant situations at work or in daily life.

Finding the Goldilocks Spot

Our goal is to induce deep processing so that learners will acquire specific skills or knowledge. But what is the appropriate amount of deep processing to require? On the one hand, if you require more deep processing than learners can comfortably do, they may be frustrated, discouraged, and fail to learn. On the other hand, if you undershoot and go too far in the other direction, requiring too little processing, they may be bored, disengaged, and fail to learn. You need to find the "Goldilocks spot," somewhere in the middle—where the amount of processing is not too much or too little, but is just right. This brings up a fundamental problem, which probably has bedeviled educators since classroom instruction began: Different learners have different Goldilocks spots. What's "just right" for Noorjit may be too hard for Anne, and what's just right for Anne may be too hard for Marie.

One way to address this problem is to assign a human tutor to each learner. The tutor is bright, well-informed, wise, and sensitive, and they adjust instruction so that it is appropriate for the individual learner. Were that we had a surplus supply of such people—and the finances to employ them! But alas, this solution does not scale.

Another way to try to deal with this problem is to program computers to mimic a gifted tutor. We can approach this goal in two ways, either by using specialized software that is designed to help learners with a particular subject or by using AI. Let's first consider the now-traditional approach, using specialized programs that do "Computer Aided Instruction," "Intelligent Computer Aided Instruction," "Adaptive Instruction," or "Personalized Learning."[40] Such programs can be useful, especially in areas where there are clear, correct answers, such as math, basic chemistry, and basic physics. However, such systems have numerous problems.[41] For one, it is sometimes possible to "game" them and get the right answers for the wrong reasons—and because there is no follow-up, no one is the wiser. But more than this, learners often simply don't want to interact with a rigid machine. They want a more social, conversational interaction.

The second computer-based approach relies on AI. One way to use AI to find the Goldilocks spot for each person is to design a prompt so that the AI initially presents information at different levels and asks the learner to select which one is most comfortable. For example, consider the learning objective "Define key terms and concepts in the context of supply and demand, such as quantity supplied, quantity demanded, equilibrium, and market-clearing price." I submitted the following prompt, and Box 5 shows how the AI responded.

---

[40] Duchastel, P., & Imbeau, J. (1988). Intelligent computer-assisted instruction (ICAI): Flexible learning through better student-computer interaction. *Journal of Information Technology, 3,* 102-105; Mann, B.L. (2009). Computer-Aided Instruction. *Wiley Online Library.* 10.1002/9780470050118. ecse935; Singhal, A. (2018). The evolving state of AI-supplemented computer-assisted instruction. *EmergingEdTech.* https://www.emergingedtech.com/2018/05/artificial-intelligence- supplemented-computer-assisted-instruction/

[41] Intelligent tutoring system. *Wikipedia:* https://en.wikipedia.org/wiki/Intelligent_tutoring_system

AI Prompt

You are playing the role of a tutor, helping a learner to master the learning objective "Define key terms and concepts in the context of supply and demand, such as quantity supplied, quantity demanded, equilibrium, and market-clearing price." Different learners prefer different levels of sophistication and complexity, so could you first please provide three versions of a summary of the first part of the learning objective, "Define key terms and concepts in the context of supply and demand, such as quantity supplied"; the different versions should be at different levels of sophistication and complexity: High, medium, and low. After you provide the three versions, ask the learner which one they prefer: the first, second, or third. After this, address the rest of the learning objective at the corresponding level.

BOX 5: Having an AI adjust the level of complexity of its responses

AI:
Sure, here are three different explanations for the concept of "quantity supplied" in the context of supply and demand.

High Complexity:
In the realm of economics, "quantity supplied" is a pivotal concept within the market dynamics and is a function of price as per the law of supply. It refers to the total number of units of a good or service that producers are willing and able to sell at a given price over a specific time period. This concept is anchored in the tenet that, other things being equal, an increase in price results in an increase in the quantity supplied, as suppliers aim to maximize profits. This relationship is typically depicted graphically through a supply curve, which is upward sloping, signifying that as price increases, the quantity of goods that suppliers are willing to produce and sell also increases.

Medium Complexity:
"Quantity supplied" is a key term in economics that deals with how much of a product or service producers are willing to sell at a certain price. It's based on the law of supply, which says that when the price of something goes up, producers are usually willing to supply more of it, because they

can make more money from it. This relationship can be represented on a graph with an upward-sloping supply curve.

Low Complexity:
"Quantity supplied" simply means how much of something people are willing to sell at a certain price. If the price is high, they usually want to sell more because they can make more money. You can think of it like a lemonade stand: if you can sell each cup of lemonade for a lot of money, you'll want to make and sell as much lemonade as you can!

Which of these explanations do you prefer? The first (high complexity), second (medium complexity), or third (low complexity)? Based on your preference, I'll proceed to explain the other concepts at a similar level.

Me:
low-level version

AI:
Alright, I'll continue with the low complexity explanations.

Quantity demanded:
This is how much of something people want to buy at a certain price. It's like how many cups of lemonade you'd want if each cup cost a dollar, versus if each cup cost five dollars. Usually, if things are cheaper, people want to buy more.

Equilibrium:
This is the sweet spot where the amount of something people want to buy (quantity demanded) and the amount people want to sell (quantity supplied) are the same. So if you're selling lemonade and you've got just the right amount that everyone who wants to buy a cup can get one, you're at equilibrium.

Market-clearing price:
This is the price where equilibrium happens. It's the price where you sell just the right amount of lemonade so that everyone who wants a cup gets one, and you don't have any left over. It's the perfect price that "clears the market" of the product.

I hope this helps! Let me know if you have any questions or if there's anything else you want to know about.

Me:
I changed my mind. High-level version, please.

AI:
Of course, let's dive into the high complexity explanations.

Quantity demanded:
In economic theory, quantity demanded refers to the total volume of a good or service that consumers are willing and able to purchase at a given price within a particular time period. According to the law of demand, there is an inverse relationship between price and quantity demanded, given that all other factors are held constant. As the price of a good rises, consumers are typically less inclined to purchase the same volume of that good, leading to a decrease in quantity demanded. Conversely, if the price of a good falls, the quantity demanded generally increases. This relationship is depicted graphically by a demand curve, which is downward sloping.

Equilibrium: Economic equilibrium is a state in a market where the quantity of a good supplied by producers equals the quantity of that good demanded by consumers. This balance ensures that there is no surplus or shortage of the good in the market. Equilibrium is achieved at a certain price and quantity, referred to as the equilibrium price and equilibrium quantity, respectively. In this state, there is no pressure on the price to either rise or fall, as the market forces of supply and demand are in balance.

Market-clearing price: The market-clearing price, also known as the equilibrium price, is the price at which the quantity supplied equals the quantity demanded. This is the price that balances the intentions of buyers and sellers, resulting in a stable market with no excess supply or unmet demand. At the market-clearing price, every consumer who is willing to buy the good at that price can do so, and every producer who is willing to sell the good at that price can do so. This price optimizes efficiency, as all units of the good that are produced are also consumed.

> I hope this provides a more in-depth understanding of these concepts. Please feel free to ask for further clarification or to delve into more complex economic principles.

As shown in Box 5, the AI nicely adjusted the level to that preferred by the learner. Another approach is to instruct the AI to begin at an intermediate level and then, after two paragraphs, ask the learner whether to make the material more complex and detailed, less complex and detailed, or keep it at the same level.

If the learner hits a spot where the material isn't clear to them, they can ask the AI to explain in more detail. In fact, they can ask for a tutorial on any part or all of the subject. The AI will not only deliver one but also will answer any questions with remarkable patience, without a trace of being judgmental. Because it can answer questions at any level, the AI can quickly adjust to the Goldilocks spot for any given learner.

But there is a fly in this ointment, at least as of this writing: As noted in Chapter 2, AIs aren't always right and sometimes make things up. To minimize AI hallucinations, the instructor needs to follow best practices when creating the prompts and provide the AI with relevant resources, especially if the material is novel, specialized, or nuanced. The prompt should clearly indicate that the AI should base its responses on these resources, and give them priority over other information it has. Following this, the instructor needs to ask the AI for tutorials for each learning objective, and ensure that the information conveyed in each one is correct.[42]

In short, you can structure an activity so that learners will engage in relevant and appropriate deep processing, which helps them achieve a specific learning outcome. If you formulate a learning objective in advance, it can guide you to design the activity so that the learners engage in the kind of processing that will achieve this end. The beauty of this approach is that the learners can master the material as a byproduct of engaging in

---

[42] The AI companies are very aware of the problem, and I expect the AIs soon to improve on this score.

mental processing, even if they are not particularly interested in learning that material. In the following chapters, we see many additional ways to induce and buttress deep processing.

Using AI to Develop Activities

You can use AI to create active learning exercises that invoke the Principle of Deep Processing by deploying the following prompt. You need to adapt the "objective" for the AI based on your learning objective and need to specify the appropriate level.[43] In addition, in this and all of the following prompts, if you are not using GPT-4, change that notation to the name of your AI.

AI Prompt

Objective: Engage in a real-time, active learning exchange about photosynthesis with a human learner. Guidelines: Interactive Dialogue: Engage in a one-on-one dialogue with the learner. Ask one question at a time and always wait for the learner's response before proceeding. Solo Activity: Ensure all interactions are only between the learner and GPT-4, or role-played entities introduced by GPT-4. Engagement Level: Make the activity engaging, fun, and novel. Focus on one learning principle: Rely on the Active Learning Principle of Deep Processing, which states: "The more mental processing one performs on information, the more likely one is to retain it; thus active learning should engage learners to pay attention to and think through material that underlies the learning objective." Example: Ask students to compare and contrast, not simply recall. Target Audience: Keep the activity at a high school level. Do Not Reference Deep Processing Principle: Avoid mentioning the Active Learning Principle of Deep Processing. Begin the activity when ready.

---

[43] This prompt, and the similar ones in the following chapters, was developed with help from GPT-4: I wrote a prompt and then submitted it to the AI, telling it the goal and asking it to improve the prompt. It inserted the headings (e.g., "Objective") and capitalized some of the words, but did not change the content substantively. I retained its capitalization conventions.

The learners are simply told to submit this prompt and then respond appropriately to the AI's questions. Box 6 shows what happened when I submitted this prompt to GPT-4. In the following four chapters, we will see what GPT-4 does when we use versions of this prompt for each of the different learning principles.

BOX 6: An example of how AI can employ the Principle of Deep Processing

AI:
Welcome to the World of Photosynthesis Adventure!
To save the land of Chlorophylla, you need to understand the magic of photosynthesis. Every step you take will be a choice. Your understanding will be the key to unlock the wonders of Chlorophylla.

You stand at the entrance of a vast and dense forest. In front of you, there's a huge leaf with a sign that reads: "Chlorophylla's Heartbeat." Before we step in, let's get to know our basics. What do you understand by photosynthesis? Just a brief idea.

[Waiting for the learner's response.]

Me:
Photosynthesis is the process by which plants use sunlight, CO-2, and water to create sugar.

AI:
Perfect!

As you give the correct answer, the entrance to the forest opens. You step onto a path lined with radiant green leaves shimmering under the sun's rays. Birds sing and you feel a gentle breeze.

Great start! But wait, the land of Chlorophylla relies on a certain green pigment that plays a pivotal role in photosynthesis. Can you name it?

[Waiting for the learner's response.]

Me:
chlorophyl

AI:
Almost right! It's chlorophyll. Just a minor spelling hiccup.
As you say the word, the leaves on the trees surrounding you glow
brightly. It seems the trees appreciate your knowledge.

You come across a glimmering pond where two types of fish are
swimming: One named "Light Reaction" and the other named "Dark
Reaction".

If you had to think of photosynthesis as a two-stage process, which fish
would represent the stage where sunlight is directly used?

[Waiting for the learner's response.]

Me:
Light reaction

AI:
Exactly right!

As you answer, the "Light Reaction" fish glows and starts leading you
through a water channel. This channel symbolizes the thylakoid
membrane of the chloroplast. As you follow the glowing fish, you see
how water molecules are split, releasing oxygen and producing energy-
rich molecules.

As you observe this fascinating process, can you tell me what gas is
released as a byproduct when water molecules are split during the light
reaction?

[Waiting for the learner's response.]

Me:
Oxygen

AI:

Correct!

As you say "oxygen", bubbles rise from the water and merge into a serene mist above the channel. Now, you find yourself on the other side of the pond. Here, the "Dark Reaction" fish is waiting.

The "Dark Reaction" fish introduces you to the next stage of photosynthesis that doesn't directly require light but uses the energy-rich molecules from the light reaction.

This mysterious part of Chlorophylla is where plants magically convert carbon dioxide into something sweet. What is this sweet thing that plants produce during the dark reaction?

[Waiting for the learner's response.]

Me:
sugar

AI:
That's right!

As you say "sugar", the path ahead of you becomes covered in sweet crystal-like structures. These represent glucose molecules. You can see that these sugars are the energy stores, the lifeblood of Chlorophylla. You've now traveled through the main stages of photosynthesis, seeing the magic of how plants harness the sun's energy and produce life-giving sugars.

Now, for a fun challenge! Imagine you're a chef in Chlorophylla. Using sunlight, water, and CO2, create a "recipe" for photosynthesis. What would be your ingredients and the final dish?

[Waiting for the learner's response.]

Me:
What do you mean by "recipe"?

AI:

Ah! I meant crafting a fun, imaginative way to describe photosynthesis as if you were creating a dish in a kitchen.

For example: Ingredients:
- A cup of sunlight
- 6 molecules of water
- 6 molecules of carbon dioxide

Instructions:
1. Take the sunlight and mix it with water in the "Light Reaction Blender" to produce oxygen, ATP, and NADPH.
2. In a separate bowl, combine ATP, NADPH, and carbon dioxide. Stir well in the "Calvin Cycle Mixer".
3. Allow the mixture to settle and voila! You have a delicious glucose dish ready to serve.

Now, how would you craft your own recipe for the photosynthesis dish?

[Waiting for the learner's response.]

Me:
Ah! That sounds pretty good. Thank you.

As you can see, the AI did a good job of inducing the learner to think about the relevant material.

Here are some examples of particular types of exercises that will draw on the Principle of Deep Processing.

- Have the AI generate a short essay that addresses the learning objective and ask the learners to evaluate it according to specific criteria. You can even ask the AI to provide the criteria, given the nature of the learning objective.

- Have the AI generate two short essays that address the learning objective and ask the learners to compare and contrast how well they address that learning objective. You can do the same thing with graphics, for relevant learning objectives.

- Ask the AI to identify the most difficult part of the reading material and ask the learners to explain why they agree or disagree that this is, in fact, the most difficult part.

- Ask the AI to reframe an essay or reading, and ask the learners to identify which version is better and explain why.

- Ask the AI to critique an essay or reading and ask the learners to agree or disagree with its analysis and explain why.

- Ask the AI to create a game to help learners achieve the learning objective and ask the learners to critique it.

- Ask the AI to quiz the learners on the relationship between the material underlying the learning objective and the material from a related learning objective that was addressed in a different class session.

In Chapter 2, I pointed out a potential problem with these sorts of activities, namely that the learners can try to avoid doing the work (and thereby circumvent active learning) by asking an AI to do the task for them. It's worth reiterating one way to address this issue: Have the AI conduct a follow-up interview immediately after the activity, where it debriefs the learners in real time. In this interview, the AI asks the learner to explain, justify, or elaborate on their responses, perhaps even asking them to reference their personal experiences—keeping in mind that they should avoid discussing private or sensitive information. I describe such a process in Chapter 11, using a rubric to ensure that the AI focuses on the relevant aspects of the learning objective. You can use this procedure with any of the activities described in this book. The key is that the learners have to respond immediately after the task and respond in real time to specific questions—and follow-up questions—that are difficult to anticipate in advance.

—5—

Chunking

Every instructor knows that it's a bad idea to present too much material in a lecture or require learners to deal with too much material in an activity. But how much is too much? Researchers have found that we humans can take in only about three or four "chunks" at a time.[44] A *chunk* is created when you organize information into a unit. To get a sense of what a chunk is, glance at the following letters for a few seconds and try to memorize them in order:

XXCBSCIAIBMNBCXX

Now look away from the letters and try to recall them. How many of the letters did you memorize after a glance?

Now try it again, but use this hint: Look for three-letter acronyms of famous organizations.

How many can you recall now?

---

[44] Cowan, N. (2001). The magical number 4 in short-term memory: A reconsideration of mental storage capacity. *Behavioral and Brain Sciences, 24*, 87–114.

Most people can use top-down processing to memorize the entire string when they look for acronyms. I could have achieved the same end by printing CBS in green, CIA in red, IBM in blue, and NBC in yellow. Or I could have achieved the same result simply by inserting a space between the groups of three letters, as in: CBS CIA IBM NBC. By adding colors or spaces, I help you use bottom-up processing to organize the individual letters into chunks (see Chapter 3).

You probably rely on chunking a lot when you are engaged in two-factor authentication. Look at these verification codes. Which ones are easiest to recall?

640815

123456

711229

116633

415617

Most people find the second, third, and fourth codes easier to recall than the first. Why? Because you can organize them into chunks, using bottom-up processing. If you are familiar with the San Francisco and Boston telephone area codes, then you will also find the last one easy to chunk, using top-down processing, given that 415 is a San Francisco area code and 617 is a Boston area code.

The real power of chunking comes from the fact that each chunk can itself contain chunks, and it's the highest-level (largest) chunk that's important for our limited capacities. For example, the number of letter strokes that go into writing a digit is not relevant (e.g., "1" has fewer strokes than "4"); the strokes are organized into a single chunk, and those digits can, in turn, be organized into larger chunks. For example, the verification code "123456" is a single chunk with six digits, whereas 415617 would be two chunks of three digits each, if you know the area codes. Our mental capacity limits are defined by the "highest level" chunks.

The Principle of Chunking states that *"Learning is easier when material is organized into three or four organized units, each of which itself can contain three or four units."* This principle applies to all types of information; for example, it can allow you to organize a list, a diagram, or a spoken lecture into chunks.

A particularly impressive example of such hierarchical chunking was reported in 1980 by a team of researchers at Carnegie Mellon University in Pittsburg.[45] They studied a single undergraduate over the course of about a year and a half. This volunteer came into the lab to be tested at least three times per week. The study was deceptively simple: The researchers read aloud a series of lists of random digits, and the participant repeated back each list. The researchers began with a list that was only one digit long. They read the digit, and the participant repeated it back. The researchers then read a list with two randomly selected digits, presented one per second, and the participant repeated the list. The researchers then presented a list with three randomly selected digits, one per second, which the participant repeated back, and the researchers continued to lengthen the list by one additional random digit until the participant no longer repeated all of them accurately. That first day, he correctly recalled lists up to seven digits long, which is average—it's typically easy to find a way to organize seven random digits into four or fewer chunks. The next session picked up where the previous one had left off, presenting a list at the maximum length recalled before (seven, on this second day). Every list was different, consisting of a new series of randomly selected digits, read one per second. The length of the lists grew steadily longer over time as the participant improved. When the researchers finally called it quits, the participant had just repeated back a new list of 79 random digits!

At the end of the very first session, the participant faltered after the list contained more than seven digits—what changed over time that allowed him eventually to recall 79 random digits? The trick was that the participant developed clever ways to organize digits into chunks and—crucially—to organize each of these individual chunks so that they, in turn,

---

[45] Ericsson, K. A., Chase, W. G., & Faloon, S. (1980). Acquisition of a memory skill. *Science, 208*, 1181- 1182.

were grouped into larger chunks. Specifically, this participant had run in numerous marathon races and recalled the time he took for various segments of these races, or he recalled times of races he ran early or late in his career. He was able to convert a set of random digits into specific times. For example, if the string of digits was "3, 4, 9, 2," he related these numbers to a time he recalled: "3 minutes and 49 point 2 seconds, near world-record mile time." (p. 1181). This strategy allowed him to replace what were four separate entities with a single chunk. He then organized sets of these segments into a larger group, perhaps reflecting segments of a particular marathon he recalled, which created an even larger chunk. As he worked out such strategies, he broadened his approach and came to organize some of the digits into specific people's ages or highly memorable dates.[46]

The results of this study illustrate two key facts about how our brains work when we are learning: The first is that we store information as organized units, not individual isolated bits; the second is that each of these units, in turn, can be part of a larger unit. The combination of these two factors allows us to process and take in an enormous amount of information.

Chunking Rules

In Chapter 3, we considered bottom-up versus top-down processing, both of which contribute to chunking. Bottom-up processing organizes chunks based on physical properties, such as sets of the same digit in a row or simple sequences in the above two-step verification codes. In contrast, top-down processing creates chunks based on knowledge (such as of acronyms or area codes).

---

[46] This finding has been replicated and extended; see, for example, Yoon, J-S., Ericsson, K. A., & Donatelli, D. (2018). Effects of 30 years of disuse on exceptional memory performance. *Cognitive Science, 42*, 884-903.

Although there are over 100 known principles that govern bottom-up chunking, we can get very far by considering only four of them:[47]

Similarity. Similar material tends to be grouped together. For example, you see 000xxx as two units, with the zeros being grouped into one unit and the x's into the other. This principle also applies to conceptual information: Similar ideas will often be chunked together.

Proximity. Nearby material tends to be grouped together. For example, you see XXX XXX as two units, not six separate Xs. In contrast, you now see the same number of Xs as four units because of how they are spaced: XX XX XX XX. Nearby Xs are chunked together. This principle applies not just in space but also in time: Material presented consecutively, for example in a lecture, tends to be grouped together, especially if pauses—the temporal equivalent of spaces—are inserted to indicate boundaries of chunks.

Symmetry. Symmetrical material tends to be grouped together. You see \\ // as a single chunk, but not \\ || , which similarity and proximity will group into two chunks. This principle also can work conceptually, for example, if an introduction and conclusion act as "bookends" to a piece.

Good continuation. Material that falls along a clear trajectory tends to be grouped together. For example, you see - - - - - - as a single unit, but you see - - - ¯ ¯ ¯ as two units. This also works conceptually. For example, 123456 is grouped as a single unit, whereas 213465 is not.

In contrast, top-down chunking relies on what you know. Such chunking often hinges on associations, such as we saw earlier for digits that correspond to different telephone area codes. We will return to this topic in the next chapter.

Critically, once you have a chunk, no matter how you created it, it acts as a single unit—and we can hold three or four such chunks at the same time in our short-term memories (and hence be conscious of them—see Chapter 3).

---

[47] For an overview of these grouping principles, as well as historical context for their discovery and application, see: https://en.wikipedia.org/wiki/Gestalt_psychology

Using AI to Chunk a Presentation

After you define your learning objectives, you may create a class session or lecture—which then feeds into how you design active learning exercises. During this initial phase, you might find it helpful to free-associate ideas and jot them down as they spring to mind. For example, imagine that you live in New York City and are thinking about what the city should do with the excess office space. Imagine that you are considering giving a lecture on this from the perspective of the "human side of things." Here is an example of the sorts of notes you might generate on the topic, in no particular order:

> What would it take to induce people to want to move into these conversions? What advantages and disadvantages would they have? Could they be cheaper than other apartments? How do we figure out what they would cost to do? Can we attract people based on sustainability? Reusing existing structures; carbon footprint reduction. Also: consider the city itself, and how to appeal to potential residents based on how it helps the city. Economic implications–how conversion can be a viable solution to handle vacant office buildings and also potentially lower the cost of urban living. Start with the context, of the covid pandemic, working from home, and reluctance to return to the office. That's led to a growing interest in "adaptive reuse," turning office buildings into residences. Practicalities: Architectural challenges in doing these conversions (e.g., typical office building characteristics don't fit residential requirements well, such as low ceiling heights, no natural light for the interior, plumbing not optimal for bathrooms or kitchens, ventilation issues). Also need to worry about residential requirements (e.g., sound insulation, privacy). Good to have examples of successful conversions; what design strategies worked? What failed? What different professionals are involved in these conversions (e.g., architects, structural engineers, interior designers)? Also would need to explore how such conversions impact the local urban fabric (e.g., can rejuvenate neighborhoods but also, perhaps, displace some people).

Now let's see how GPT-4 can employ the principles of chunking to organize this material, based on the prompt in Box 7. As you can see, the AI did a good job of pulling together the somewhat random information I gave it.

BOX 7: Using chunking rules to organize a presentation

Me:
After "1:" is a set of rules of chunking. Please use these rules to organize the material that follows after "2:". When you organize, have no more than four "chunks" at the top level, and then use hierarchical organization to ensure that there are no more than four entries at each level under the major headings.

1. (a) Similarity. Similar material tends to be grouped together. For example, similar ideas will often be chunked together. (b) Proximity. Nearby material tends to be grouped together. For example, material presented consecutively (e.g., in a lecture) tends to be grouped together. (c) Symmetry. Symmetrical material tends to be grouped together. This principle also can work conceptually, for example if an introduction and conclusion act as "bookends" to a piece. (d) Good continuation. Material that falls along a clear trajectory tends to be grouped together. For example, 123456 is grouped as a single unit, whereas 213465 is not. 5) Previously stored associations can be used to group material into a chunk.
2. [I inserted my notes here]

AI:
Based on the rules provided, I would organize the given information into the following categories:

I. Context and Motivations
   A. COVID pandemic and shift to working from home
   B. Growing interest in adaptive reuse
   C. Addressing urban vacancies and reducing cost of living

II. Practical Considerations for Conversions
   A. Architectural Challenges
      1. Office buildings' characteristics don't fit residential requirements

      2. Inadequate plumbing and ventilation for residential use
      3. Need for sound insulation and privacy
   B. Involved Professionals
      1. Architects
      2. Structural engineers
      3. Interior designers
   C. Examples of successful conversions
      1. What design strategies worked
      2. What strategies failed

III. Potential Benefits and Appeals
   A. Sustainability
      1. Reusing existing structures
      2. Reduction of carbon footprint
   B. Affordability
      1. Possibility of conversions being cheaper than other apartments
   C. City Advantages
      1. Revitalization of neighborhoods
      2. Positive impacts on the city's economy

IV. Potential Disadvantages and Concerns
   A. Displacement of existing residents
   B. Potential downsides of conversions

GPT-4 clearly drew on the chunking rules I provided: It grouped together similar content (similarity), it presented content on related themes consecutively (proximity), it had each chunk follow a clear trajectory (good continuation), and it arranged the chunks to form a coherent symmetrical structure, with the introduction (noting upsides) and conclusion (noting downsides) acting as conceptual bookends (symmetry). It also structured the material to respect previously stored associations, such as the link between architectural challenges and involved professions (stored associations used in top-down processing).

You can also employ the Principle of Chunking to determine how much material you put on a single slide in a lecture, how many activities you present in a class, and practically anything else that involves organizing some kind of components. In all cases, the idea is to organize the materials so that they are as simple as possible—but, to paraphrase Albert Einstein, no simpler than that. You should ensure that learners don't need to take in more than three or four overarching chunks when viewing a slide, reading instructions, using a diagram, and so on—and each of these overarching chunks should contain no more than three or four sub-chunks.[48]

Using AI to Develop Activities

You can use AI to create active learning exercises that invoke the Principle of Chunking, for example by relying on a version of the prompt we employed at the end of the previous chapter. Again, you need to adapt the instructions so that the "objective" to the AI fits your learning objective and you need specify the appropriate level.

AI Prompt

Objective: Engage in a real-time, active learning exchange about the distinctive elements of the Beatles' music with a human learner. Guidelines: Interactive Dialogue: Engage in a one-on-one dialogue with the learner. Ask one question at a time and always wait for the learner's response before proceeding. Solo Activity: Ensure all interactions are only between the learner and GPT-4, or role-played entities introduced by GPT-4. Engagement Level: Make the activity engaging, fun, and novel. Focus on one learning principle: Rely on the Active Learning Principle of Chunking, which states: "Learning is easier when material is organized into three or four organized units, each of which itself can contain three or four units; this principle can be used to organize entire lessons into units but also operates at more granular levels." Example: No more than three organized groups of text should be presented on a single slide during a presentation. Target Audience: Keep the activity at a college level. Do Not

---

[48] Cf. Chandler, P., & Sweller, J. (1991). Cognitive load theory and the format of instruction. *Cognition and Instruction, 8*, 293-332.

Reference Chunking Principle: Avoid mentioning the Active Learning Principle of Chunking. Begin the activity when ready.

Box 8 shows how GPT-4 responded to that prompt—and, again, the instructions to the learners simply ask them to respond to the AI's questions.

BOX 8: An example of how AI can employ the Principle of Chunking

AI:
Alright, let's dive into our exploration of the Beatles' music, a band known for their innovation in popular music. For this journey, think of yourself as an archaeologist sifting through layers of musical history. We'll break this down into three main "layers" or aspects to make it easier to digest:

1. Their musical style and innovation
2. The lyrical content and storytelling
3. The band's evolution and impact

Are you ready to start digging into the first layer - their musical style and innovation?

Me:
Yes!

AI:
Great! Let's start with the Beatles' musical style and innovation. Their music is known for its extraordinary diversity and innovation.

Genre-blending: The Beatles were known for blending genres in innovative ways. They started with rock 'n' roll and pop, but quickly incorporated elements of classical music, folk, blues, and even Indian music. Can you think of a Beatles song that incorporates elements from a genre outside of rock 'n' roll?

Studio Experimentation: The Beatles were pioneers in using the studio as an instrument. They used multi-tracking, innovative microphone placements, and played around with effects like reverb and delay. Do you know any Beatles songs that are famous for their studio techniques? Harmonic Creativity: The Beatles utilized interesting chord progressions, key changes, and harmonies which were quite advanced for pop music of their era. This musical complexity is often hidden by the catchy, accessible surface of their songs. Can you name a Beatles song that stands out to you in terms of its harmonies or chord progressions?

Me:
1.   Tomorrow Never Knows; 2. Today and Tomorrow. 3. A Day in the Life

AI:
Excellent choices!

"Tomorrow Never Knows" is a prime example of the Beatles' genre-blending. The song is heavily influenced by Indian music, specifically the drone-based nature of Indian classical music. It's a testament to their willingness to experiment and incorporate non-Western musical forms into their work.

"Strawberry Fields Forever" (assuming you meant this instead of "Today and Tomorrow" which is not a Beatles song) is famous for its innovative studio techniques. The final version of the song is actually a blend of two different takes, recorded in different keys and tempos. Producer George Martin and engineer Geoff Emerick came up with the revolutionary idea to speed up one take and slow down the other to match them together. "A Day in the Life" is indeed a standout in terms of its harmonic complexity. It features an orchestral build-up that blurs the lines between pop and classical music, and the song itself is a blend of two distinct song ideas from Lennon and McCartney, showcasing their unique songwriting partnership.

Now that we've explored their musical style and innovation, let's move on to the next layer: The Beatles' lyrical content and storytelling. Ready to continue?

Me:
Yes

AI:
Fantastic! Let's delve into the lyrical content and storytelling in the Beatles' music. They moved from simple love songs to more complex and profound lyrics as their career progressed.

Early Love Songs: In their early career, the Beatles' lyrics often centered around love and relationships, with straightforward, yet catchy and relatable messages. An example is "She Loves You," which is still one of their most popular songs. Can you recall another early Beatles' song that deals with love or relationships?

Social Commentary: As the Beatles matured, they began to incorporate more social commentary into their lyrics. Songs like "Eleanor Rigby" and "A Day in the Life" provide commentary on the human condition and societal issues. Can you think of another Beatles song that includes elements of social commentary?

Abstract and Experimental: In their late career, the Beatles' lyrics became more abstract and experimental, often influenced by psychedelic experiences or philosophical ideas. "Strawberry Fields Forever" and "I Am the Walrus" are examples of this. Can you think of another Beatles' song with abstract or experimental lyrics?

Me:
1.   I Want to Hold Your Hand. 2. Nowhere Man. 3. Hey Bulldog

AI:
Great picks!

"I Want to Hold Your Hand" is a perfect example of the Beatles' early love songs. It's simple, catchy, and filled with youthful enthusiasm, and it was indeed the song that triggered "Beatlemania" in the United States. "Nowhere Man" is a great example of the Beatles' social commentary. The song is a reflection on identity and alienation, showing a departure from their early love songs and marking a new direction in their songwriting.

"Hey Bulldog" is indeed more abstract and experimental. The song is known for its nonsensical lyrics and playful, surreal imagery, showing the

Beatles' willingness to push the boundaries of what could be done in a pop song.

Now, let's explore the final layer: The Beatles' evolution and impact. Ready to move on?

Me:
Yes

AI:
Great! Now let's explore The Beatles' evolution and impact. The Beatles' career, although just a decade long, was marked by a continuous evolution in their music, influencing generations of artists and reshaping popular music.

The Early Years: The Beatles started as a skiffle band playing in Liverpool and Hamburg. Their early music was influenced by rock 'n' roll and pop artists like Chuck Berry and Buddy Holly. Can you name a song from their early years that reflects these influences?

The Middle Years: This period is marked by increasing musical sophistication and experimentation, both lyrically and musically. They started exploring different genres and using the studio in innovative ways. Can you think of a song from this period that represents their musical growth?

The Late Years: In their late career, the Beatles' music became more eclectic and experimental. Their lyrics became more abstract, often influenced by psychedelic experiences and philosophical ideas. Can you name a song from their late years that reflects these changes?

This journey will help us understand how The Beatles reshaped the landscape of popular music and continue to influence artists today.

Me:
1.   I Saw Her Standing There. 2. Strawberry Fields Forever. 3. I can't think of one...

AI:
Good job!

"I Saw Her Standing There" is indeed a great example of the Beatles' early rock 'n' roll influences. The song's energetic rhythm and catchy melody are reminiscent of the popular music styles of the late 50s and early 60s.

"Strawberry Fields Forever" is a fantastic example of their middle period. The song's innovative studio techniques, the blending of different takes, and the psychedelic lyrics mark a clear shift from their earlier works. Not to worry about the third one! An example of a late Beatles song could be "Across the Universe". The lyrics are philosophical and abstract, and the use of the Indian sitar reflects their ongoing experimentation with different musical styles and instruments.

We've now completed our journey through the three layers of the Beatles' music: their musical style and innovation, the lyrical content and storytelling, and the band's evolution and impact. Do you have any questions or is there anything else you'd like to explore further about the Beatles?

That interaction with the AI clearly involved chunking, and also required quite a bit of deep processing. Here are some examples of particular types of exercises that draw on the Principle of Chunking. In each case, you can give the AI a rubric and ask it to grade the learners' responses (see Chapter 11).

- Have the learners listen to a lecture and ask them to organize it into chunks. The AI grades the learners based on how many chunks they correctly identified.

- Give the AI a properly formatted document and ask it to create three versions: one version is parsed incorrectly rarely; another is parsed incorrectly occasionally; and the third is parsed incorrectly frequently. You then ask the learners to evaluate the chunking in each version, identifying errors. The AI then provides feedback.

- Have the AI provide examples of materials organized according to different principles, and ask the learners to identify the specific chunking principle(s) at work; the AI scores the learners.

- Enter a document into the AI and instruct it to organize the document in three different ways. The learners then select the best one and justify their judgment.

—6—

Building
Associations

The Principle of Associations states that *"Learning is enhanced by associating new information to what is already known."* Associations are so powerful and so pervasive that this principle is often employed in conjunction with other active learning principles. For example, many associations require deep processing. However, associations can boost learning in their own right, without drawing on the other principles.

Associations play a key role in three different phases of learning: In organizing and interpreting material during the initial phase, in storing and retaining it, and in digging material out of long-term memory when it needs to be used.

Associations in Organizing and Interpreting

In the previous chapter, I slipped in examples of the power of associations in organizing to-be-learned material. The first example was the chunks you created at the outset of that chapter, where you associated letters with familiar acronyms (such as IBM and CBS), followed by the example of how to apply knowledge of telephone area codes to organize two-factor verification codes. If you had not already associated those letters or digits together into chunks and stored those chunks in your long-term memory, you couldn't have used them to organize the strings of letters or digits. You relied on the previous associations to organize the new material. Another example was the remarkable case of the person who was able to memorize 79 random digits, read aloud one digit every second. In the previous chapter, I emphasized the fact that he had constructed chunks based largely on his knowledge of the times he required to run segments of marathon races. I noted but didn't emphasize the fact that he was using prior associations to create these chunks.

Hierarchical Learning Objectives

The Principle of Associations implies that we should begin with foundational material that engenders associations that organize everything else. This idea leads us to define learning objectives at several levels of granularity. To begin, you formulate the overarching learning objective or objectives for each unit, which can link everything you discuss in the individual lessons within them. Following this, you formulate more specific learning objectives that you want the learners to achieve in the individual lessons, and indicate how they are related. For example, your overarching learning objective might be "Identify what we can learn from the Covid-19 pandemic that could help us in the next pandemic." The more specific learning objectives might require the learners to analyze how the virus is transmitted, ways to minimize transmission (social distancing, masks, hand washing), the efficacy of vaccines, the roots of vaccine hesitancy, and the pandemic's effects on the economy, on international trade, and on immigration. You also explicitly note the connections among these factors, both the direct connections (e.g., how disruption of international trade impaired the economy) and indirect ones (e.g., how disruption of international trade affected attitudes about immigration via the tightening economy). As the course designer or instructor, it's useful to try—however imperfectly—to put yourself in the learners' shoes and take their perspective, thinking about how they might associate the different parts of the unit and each constituent lesson.

You can recruit AI to help you distill and organize learning objectives hierarchically. For example, I used the following prompt:

I want you to distill the learning objectives that are being addressed in the course I describe at the end of this prompt. Learning objectives should not use the verbs "learn," "understand," or "explore" but rather should rely on active verbs that produce behaviors that can be measured. Please make the learning objectives short and crisp. Moreover, I want you to organize the learning objectives hierarchically, indicating which ones are superordinate and which ones fall under those higher-level learning objectives. Try to put as many appropriate entries as possible under each general learning objective. The description of the course is as follows:

Course Title: Introduction to Psychology (PSYCH 101)

Course Description:

Introduction to Psychology (PSYCH 101) is a comprehensive, foundational course designed to provide students with a broad understanding of the diverse field of psychology. This course will explore the scientific study of the human mind and behavior, delving into the principles, theories, and research methods that have shaped the discipline. Students will gain insight into a range of topics, including the biological bases of behavior, learning and memory, human development, cognition and language, motivation and emotion, personality, social psychology, abnormal psychology, and mental health and psychotherapy. By examining the biological, cognitive, and social processes that underlie human thought, emotion, and action, students will foster an appreciation for the complexity of human behavior.

Box 9 presents what I got. As is evident, GPT-4 produced a clear and coherent outline. Notice that it is using principles of chunking based on relevant associations.

BOX 9: Using AI to create a hierarchically organized lesson plan

AI:
Course Title: Introduction to Psychology (PSYCH 101)

Superordinate Learning Objective 1: Examine the foundations of psychology
1.1. Identify key principles and theories in psychology
1.2. Describe the scientific methods used in psychological research
1.3. Recognize the historical development of the field

Superordinate Learning Objective 2: Investigate the biological bases of behavior
2.1. Explain the role of the nervous system in human behavior
2.2. Discuss the relationship between genetics and behavior
2.3. Evaluate the effects of drugs on psychological processes

Superordinate Learning Objective 3: Analyze learning and memory processes
3.1. Compare different types of learning
3.2. Examine factors influencing memory formation
3.3. Assess strategies for improving memory retention

Superordinate Learning Objective 4: Assess human development across the lifespan
4.1. Describe stages of cognitive development
4.2. Examine social and emotional development
4.3. Investigate the impact of culture on human development

Superordinate Learning Objective 5: Evaluate cognition and language
5.1. Analyze problem-solving and decision-making processes
5.2. Discuss theories of language acquisition
5.3. Assess the role of culture in shaping cognition and language

Superordinate Learning Objective 6: Investigate motivation and emotion
6.1. Identify factors influencing motivation
6.2. Discuss theories of emotion
6.3. Analyze the relationship between motivation and emotion

Superordinate Learning Objective 7: Examine personality theories and assessment
7.1. Compare major personality theories
7.2. Evaluate methods of personality assessment
7.3. Analyze the role of genetics and environment in personality development

Superordinate Learning Objective 8: Explore social psychology concepts
8.1. Investigate the influence of social factors on human behavior
8.2. Analyze group dynamics and conformity
8.3. Evaluate theories of prejudice and discrimination

Superordinate Learning Objective 9: Understand abnormal psychology and mental health
9.1. Identify symptoms and causes of psychological disorders
9.2. Discuss methods for assessing and diagnosing psychological disorders
9.3. Evaluate various approaches to psychotherapy and mental health treatment

Clearly, this is a great place to start. The structure is accurate, as are the specific topics it suggests. You might want to move some of the sections and perhaps make some additional distinctions, such as, among different types of memory, but the AI has provided a good foundation on which to build.

Organizing Examples

An important role of the Principle of Associations is to help learners interpret the material. You can make abstract material much more comprehensible and memorable by providing examples. An AI can help you find and create examples—including illustrations that capture key aspects of the material.

You also can flip this procedure on its ear. Instead of providing the principle that ties together a set of examples or other material (e.g., observations, facts, concepts), you can have an AI present disconnected examples or other material and ask the learners to organize them into a coherent whole—and then to explain the rationale for their organization in real time, which will discourage them from having another AI do the work for them. The AI can then evaluate both how well the learners organized the material and how well they explained their rationale. An added benefit of such active learning is that learners will engage in deep processing and chunking of the relevant information—which will help them learn the associations.

Asking an AI to generate stories can also help learners develop associations that organize and interpret examples.[49] For instance, say that the learning objective is to compare and contrast the economies of the United States versus Germany just prior to World War I. One way to address this learning objective is to ask the AI to write a story about two companies, one in each country, that were engaged in a trade deal. You tell the AI to create the story to illustrate key similarities and key differences in how the economies worked. You then ask the learners to evaluate how well the AI did, pointing out what it missed or should have emphasized more.

Mental Models

We sometimes associate new information to a *mental model*. A mental model is a previously stored image or description that allows us to interpret the world and anticipate subsequent events.[50] Mental models are often based on analogies. For example, we might use a description of a boxing match as a model for understanding a political debate, looking for feints, strategic retreats, and attempts at knock-out blows. Donald

---

[49] The power of stories is reviewed in Willingham, D. T. (2004, Summer). The privileged status of story. *Ask the Cognitive Scientist*,
https://www.aft.org/ae/summer2004/willingham

[50] Al-Diban, S. (2012). Mental models. In N.M. Seel (Ed.), *Encyclopedia of the sciences of learning.* Springer, Boston, MA. https://doi.org/10.1007/978-1-4419-1428-6; Gentner, D., & Stevens, A. L. (Eds.), (1983/2014). *Mental models.* New York: Psychology Press; Holtrop, J.S., Scherer, L.D., Matlock, D.D., Glasgow, R.E., & Green, L.A. (2021). The importance of mental models in implementation science. *Frontiers of Public Health,* 9:680316. doi: 10.3389/fpubh.2021.680316

Norman, one of the fathers of Cognitive Science, gives a great example of a mental model that is based on how we describe objects or events, and how a faulty classification can lead us astray[51]: When many people walk into a room that's too cold, they may turn up the thermostat to near 100 degrees, hoping to warm up the room quickly. Why? They have a mental model of a thermostat as a valve—the more you open it, the more heat comes through. But in fact, they have described it incorrectly: a thermostat is a kind of switch—not a valve—that turns on the furnace until a certain temperature is reached, which then turns it off.

AIs apparently can use mental models if they were trained on them, but they cannot easily create new mental models on the fly. It may be useful to think of AIs as performing something like what Nobel-prize winner Daniel Kahneman[52] calls "System 1" processing, the fast, parallel, unconscious and automatic sort of processing that guides most of our everyday actions. To build a new mental model, you usually need what Kahneman calls "System 2" processing, the slow, serial, conscious and deliberate processing that relies on working memory. The new AIs don't have working memory, and hence cannot easily create new mental models. This failure may explain some of the deficiencies of AIs.[53]

Some learning theorists have gone so far as to argue that all teaching should be designed to help learners develop accurate mental models.[54] However, this goal may be appropriate for some learning objectives but

---

[51] Norman, D. A. (2013). *The design of everyday things (revised edition).* New York: Basic Books

[52] Kahneman, D. (2011). *Thinking fast and slow.* New York: Farrar, Straus and Giroux

[53] Researchers have documented failures of GPT-4 to reason correctly about novel "real world" physical situations that apparently require creating specific mental models. See Wang, K. D., Burkholder, E., Wieman, C., Salehi, S., & Haber, N. (2023, 21 September). Examining the potential and pitfalls of ChatGPT in science and engineering problem-solving. Stanford University preprint.

[54] Belcher, N. (2022, Feb 18). Learning, fast and slow. *Better Humans.* https://betterhumans.pub/learning-fast-and-slow-a364bf384c6c

not others. In particular, mental models are difficult to use when the learning objective focuses on:

1. **Complex or dynamic systems.** Mental models typically require simplifying, but some systems cannot be reduced to simple mental models. For example, no existing mental model can successfully predict the stock market or the weather.

2. **Novel situations and paradigm shifts.** Mental models are based on prior experience, and hence may not apply to something really new to us. For example, our mental models for understanding humor may leave us confused when we go to a different country.

3. **Situation-specific applications.** Many applications of skills or knowledge require taking context into account and adjusting what we do accordingly. Mental models are limited in how well they can help us adjust skills or knowledge to fit a specific situation. For example, although the mental model of a political debate as a boxing match may help us understand the debate among candidates for elected office, it may fail to illuminate a political debate in a graduate course on government policy.

These limitations should make us cautious about applying mental models in fields such as population dynamics, economics, international relations, environmental science and sustainability, quantum physics, meteorology, and medicine. In contrast, mental models are often effective in situations where the learning objective focuses on deterministic systems that will not suffer from being simplified, such as how a thermostat actually works and real-world "Newtonian" physical situations.

Associations in Storing and Retaining

The power of using associations during learning extends far beyond their role in organizing and interpreting information. Associations can also help learners integrate what they are learning into what they already know, which makes the information "stick" in memory.

Here's a nice demonstration of how using associations can help people store new information.[55] Researchers read learners the passage below and then asked them to recall it. The trick of the study was that half of the participants got the passage cold, with no title, whereas the other half first got a title that helped them associate the material with what they already knew. Here is the passage:

> "The procedure is actually quite simple. First you arrange things into different groups... Of course, one pile may be sufficient depending on how much there is to do. If you have to go somewhere else due to lack of facilities that is the next step, otherwise you are pretty well set. It is important not to overdo any particular endeavor. That is, it is better to do too few things at once than too many. In the short run this may not seem important, but complications from doing too many can easily arise. A mistake can be expensive as well... At first the whole procedure will seem complicated. Soon, however, it will become just another facet of life. It is difficult to foresee any end to the necessity for this task in the immediate future, but then one never can tell. After the procedure is completed one arranges the materials into different groups again. Then they can be put into their appropriate places. Eventually they will be used once more and the whole cycle will have to be repeated. However, that is part of life."

Most of the participants in the group that did not receive the title had difficulty even understanding the passage and performed poorly when later asked to recall it. In contrast, the participants in the group that received the title "Washing Clothes" did well—they recalled close to twice as much as the other group. Why? The title led them to associate the individual items with facts and events that they already knew.

The role of associations in helping learners store new information in long-term memory explains what some researchers thought of as a paradox: The more you know about a topic, the easier it is to learn even

---

[55] Bransford, J., & Johnson. M. (1972). Contextual prerequisites for understanding: Some investigations of comprehension and recall. *Journal of Verbal Learning & Verbal Behavior, 11*, 717–726. The passage is on p. 722.

more about it.[56] This fact can seem paradoxical if you think of long-term memory like a very large filing cabinet—which leads to the intuition that the more it is filled, the less space there is for something new. However, it's better to think of memory a web made of elastic strands: Every time you attach a new piece of information to it, the web stretches out, making room for even more connections and additional information.[57]

Associations in Accessing

Associations can also help us retrieve information from long-term memory when we need it. For example, have you ever had difficulty remembering the names of people you meet? If so, here's a simple technique that can help: When you meet someone—say someone named Sam—and want to learn their name, immediately think of another person you already know who has the same name. Then look for facial features of the new person that remind you of those of your previous acquaintance. For instance, they might have similar eyebrows or cheekbones. Then associate this feature or features with both people, the new and the familiar, and their names. This process is like that used in the "Washing Clothes" example we just considered—you are finding a way to integrate new material into what you already know. Once you do this, you have set up the "retrieval cues" that will help you later recall the person's name: When you later see that new person, just scan over their face until you hit on the feature or features that remind you of that familiar acquaintance who has the same name, which then will allow you to recall the name of your more recent acquaintance. The associations you created when you first learned the person's name thus can help you later to recall it.

In this example, you would have engaged in active learning: You first actively recalled someone else with the same name, searched for shared

---

[56] Reder, L. M., & Anderson, J. R. (1980). A partial resolution of the paradox of interference: The role of integrating knowledge. *Cognitive Psychology, 12*, 447–472; Smith, E. E., Adams, N., & Schorr, D. (1978). Fact retrieval and the paradox of interference. *Cognitive Psychology, 10*, 438–464.

[57] This analogy was suggested by GPT-4.

features that later will remind you of the connection, and then stored the associations in memory. The Principle of Deep Processing again applies here, but now in the context of cementing new associations that you have set up to help you later recall the information.

Spaced Practice and Varied Context

Spaced practice, sometimes called *distributed practice*, is practice that is spread out over time, as opposed to *mass practice*, which is cramming all in one go. Anyone who has painted old furniture quickly learns the truth of the old adage that "two thin coats are better than one thick coat." The same is true for learning: People learn more effectively when they spread practice out over time.[58]

Spaced practice is effective in part because it allows learners to associate different contexts with the same material, which later provides more possible cues to help them recall that material. Here's a vivid demonstration of the role of cues in recall: [59] Researchers asked participants to learn words either while sitting on the shore or while in scuba gear, 20 feet underwater. They later tested the participants' memory for the words either in the same situation where they learned the words or in the other situation. The results were dramatic: The participants recalled about 50% more words when they learned and recalled the words in the same situation, either both on land or both underwater. Switching contexts between learning and testing resulted in much poorer recall.

What's going on here? When we dig something out of memory, we rely on cues to help us locate that information—this is the key to the

---

[58] Custers, E.J. (2010). Long term retention of basic science knowledge: A review study. *Advances in Health Science Education, 15*, 109–128; Kooloos, J. G. M., Bergman, E. M., Scheffers, M. A. G. P., Schepens-Franke, A. N., & Vostenbosch, A. T. M. (2019). The effect of passive and active education methods applied in repetition activities on the retention of anatomical knowledge. *Anatomical Sciences Education, 13*, 458-466; Spaced repetition. *Wikipedia*: https://en.wikipedia.org/wiki/Spaced_repetition

[59] Godden, D. R., & Baddeley, A. D. (1975). Context-dependent memory in two natural environments: On land and underwater. *British Journal of Psychology, 66*, 325-331.

method for learning the names of new acquaintances I described earlier. When learners acquire new information, they associate it with the context in which they learned it. The context includes not just the physical surroundings—such as being on land or underwater—but also factors such as the learners' physical and emotional state, thoughts, desires and expectations. And because they associate these factors with what they are learning, it's later easier for them to dig the information out of memory when they are in the presence of the associated factors, which provide cues to jog their memory.

The land/underwater study demonstrates what happens when a very salient context is associated with learned material. The goal of spaced practice is to avoid the situation illustrated by this study—to easily recall information in many different situations, not just the single one where the learners acquired the information.

A simple way to have learners engage in spaced practice is to include a quick quiz at the end of every class, which includes five or six questions—and have one or two of them randomly drawn from a prior lesson, addressing a learning objective that was covered before. Requiring learners to recall earlier material repeatedly over time will lead them to form new associations that can later be used during recall.

You can, of course, use AI to help you create such quizzes. If you give it the list of learning objectives for the entire course, along with the dates when they will be introduced, it can generate a new quiz for each week. Moreover, you can prompt it to create the quizzes based primarily on the current material but also with a specified number of questions that address previous learning objectives.

You can boost the benefits of spaced practice by intentionally having learners absorb new knowledge or skills in very different contexts; doing so creates more associations that the learner later can draw on to access stored information. One way to create multiple contexts is simple: Have AI create different active learning exercises that cover the same material, which you assign as homework. These exercises need not be very long, but they should be clearly different (Chapter 11 offers many choices). You can use a modified version of the prompt at the end of Chapter 4 to specify the type of activity.

Inducing Emotion

Another way to provide contextual cues is by inducing emotion, which learners can easily associate with information to aid later recall. [60] However, it's best to use only mild emotions in this way. Although the literature contains mixed findings, some evidence suggests that strong negative emotions can actually interfere with learning.[61] Box 10 presents an example of how to prompt an AI to induce mild emotion that is associated with a learning objective. You again would ask the learners simply to respond to the AI's questions.

BOX 10: Using AI to design a vignette that produces a mild emotion

Me:
The learning objective is: "Explain the process of annealing in metallurgy." The level of learner is high school. Produce a short vignette that addresses that learning objective, at the specified level, that will induce a relatively mild positive emotion, such as happiness, in the user; please involve the user in the vignette (make it in the "second person"). Then do the same thing, but produce a short vignette that will induce in the user a relatively mild negative emotion, such as guilt.

AI:
Positive Emotion – Happiness

---

[60] McGaugh, J.L. (2003). *Memory and emotion: The making of lasting memories*. New York: Columbia University Press

[61] For example, see Lang, A. Newhangen, J., & Reeves, B. (1996). Negative video as structure: Emotion, attention, capacity, and memory. *Journal of Broadcasting and Electronic Media, 40*, 460- 477 (as cited in Schwartz, D. L., Tsang, J. M., & Blair, K. P. (2016). *The ABCs of how we learn: 26 scientifically proven approaches, how they work, and when to use them*. New York: W.W. Norton, p. 311.)

Imagine stepping into a quiet, warm blacksmith shop. The air smells of hot metal and burning wood. You're here today to learn about a beautiful process in metallurgy called annealing.

In your hands, you hold a piece of cold, hard steel. It feels heavy, inflexible, and unyielding. But you're about to change that. With the guidance of the blacksmith, you place it in the forge. The forge roars to life, and the steel becomes glowing hot. This is the first step in annealing: heating the metal. You are taking the steel up to a specific temperature, around 700°C to 900°C for steel, which is known as the "recrystallization temperature."

After the metal has been heated, it's time for the next step: cooling. However, it's not a rapid process. This metal needs to cool slowly. You watch as the blacksmith places the hot metal into a bed of ash to insulate it and reduce the cooling rate.

Why does this matter? Because annealing alters the metal's internal structure. It helps realign the crystals inside the metal, relieving stresses and making it more ductile, more workable. Tomorrow, when you return to the shop, you'll find that same piece of steel, now cool, has transformed. It's softer, more flexible, and ready to be shaped into whatever you desire. Isn't metallurgy wonderful?

Negative Emotion – Guilt

You've been given a project, an important one from your metalwork teacher. You're to shape a piece of steel into a beautiful ornament. You've been learning about annealing, a process that could make your task easier.

You start by heating the steel in a furnace. You know it needs to reach its recrystallization temperature—somewhere between 700°C and 900°C for steel—where the heat begins to alter its internal structure, relieving stresses and realigning the crystals inside the metal.

But you're eager. You've got other things to do—homework for other classes, plans with friends. You don't want to wait for the steel to cool slowly, the way annealing requires. So, you make a decision. You pull the

> glowing hot steel from the furnace and plunge it into water, ignoring the proper annealing process.
>
> The next day, you find the steel is hard, brittle. It cracks under your tools, resisting your attempts to shape it. Now you remember the importance of the slow cooling phase in annealing, which would have made the metal more ductile, easier to work with. You feel a pang of guilt. If only you had been patient and respected the process of annealing, you wouldn't be staring at a broken piece of steel now.

As you can see, this response doesn't really induce much emotion. But you can make good use of this failing: Specifically, you can send the transcript in Box 10 plus the following instructions to learners:

Instructions to the Learner

Learning is enhanced when you associate information with different emotions. One way to do this is to ask AI to generate vignettes that induce a mild emotion in the reader as they address a particular learning objective. Attached is an example of such a prompt and the results. As you can see, the results are only middling. The goal is to help learners achieve the learning objective. Can you improve the prompt to make the results more compelling? Please do not try to induce strong emotions, which can overwhelm the content. Stick to the learning objective and level, and try to improve the prompt so that the vignettes more successfully induce mild positive or negative emotions in ways that will help learners to achieve the learning objective—that is the goal here!

You then have learners submit their responses to the AI, which evaluates them based on a rubric where "best" means that it is most likely to induce emotion to help learners achieve the learning objective. However, this is a tricky assessment even for humans, which we can again turn into a strength: After the learners receive the feedback from the AI, they would be asked to evaluate that feedback, indicating why it does or does not seem compelling. These evaluations can then be graded.

Using AI to Develop Activities

You can instruct an AI to create active learning exercises that invoke the Principle of Associations by using a version of the prompt we submitted at the end of Chapter 4. Again, you need to modify the prompt so that the objective for the AI grows out of the learning objective, and you need to specify the appropriate level.

AI Prompt

Objective: Engage in a real-time, active learning exchange with a human learner about the tradeoffs between living on a farm versus living in a city. Guidelines: Interactive Dialogue: Engage in a one-on-one dialogue with the learner. Ask one question at a time and always wait for the learner's response before proceeding. Solo Activity: Ensure all interactions are only between the learner and GPT-4, or role-played entities introduced by GPT-4. Engagement Level: Make the activity engaging, fun, and novel. Focus on one learning principle: Rely on the Active Learning Principle of Associations, which states: "Learning is enhanced by associating new information to what is already known; appropriate associations can help learners to organize material effectively when encoding it, integrating it into what they already know, and retrieving it." Example: Telling people to memorize names of new faces by thinking of someone else who has the same name and then identifying common features in the new and familiar faces. Target Audience: Keep the activity at a college level. Do Not Reference Associations Principle: Avoid mentioning the Active Learning Principle of Associations. Begin the activity when ready.

Box 11 shows what I got when I gave that prompt to GPT-4:

Box 11: An example of how AI can employ the Principle of Associations

AI:
Sure, let's dive into the topic of city life versus farm life.

First, let's think about what you already know. Can you list some characteristics or features that come to mind when you think about city living?

Me:
Museums, cafes, lots of traffic, polluted, crowded, exciting

AI:
Great list! City life indeed tends to be bustling and vibrant, with numerous cultural and social opportunities like museums and cafes, albeit at the cost of higher pollution and crowding.

Now, let's shift gears a bit. What comes to mind when you think about life on a farm?

Me:
Relaxing, hard physical labor, fixing machines, clean air, taking care of animals

AI:
Well done! Farm life often involves a more hands-on, labor-intensive lifestyle, with benefits like clean air and closer contact with animals.

Now, let's take a deeper dive. Think about the feeling of excitement you mentioned about city life. Can you think of any aspects of farm life that might also be exciting or offer a different kind of thrill?

Me:
Seeing the fruits of your labor during harvest time is probably pretty gratifying

AI:
Absolutely! The satisfaction of a successful harvest can be a unique form of excitement and achievement in farm life.

Now, let's create a connection in the opposite direction. You mentioned hard physical labor as a part of farm life. Can you think of any instances where city life might also demand physical exertion or hard work?

Me:

Fixing your car

AI:
Good point! Whether it's fixing a car, biking or walking to work, or even moving furniture in an apartment, city life can indeed involve its share of physical activity.

Switching gears again, let's consider the clean air of the farm. Can you think of a place in the city where you might also experience clean air or a similar sense of tranquility?

Me:
A large park

AI:
Exactly! Large parks in cities often offer a breath of fresh air and tranquility amidst the hustle and bustle.

Now, let's flip that around. You mentioned cafes as a characteristic of city life. Can you think of a similar social or communal gathering place in a farm setting?

Me:
No

AI:
No problem at all! In a rural or farm setting, one might find that gathering places could be local farmers' markets, barn dances, county fairs, or even a neighbor's kitchen table.

Let's wrap up our discussion. Do you feel like you have a better understanding of the trade-offs between city and farm life now? And did you find drawing connections between the two helpful?

Me:
Yes, thank you

AI:
You're welcome! I'm glad to hear that you found the discussion helpful. Remember, these kinds of connections can be applied to many different

learning scenarios. Keep up the great work, and don't hesitate to reach out if you have more questions in the future. Happy learning!

The AI clearly drew on the Principle of Associations when conducting the discussion. Here are some additional examples of particular types of exercises that draw on this principle. In each case, you can give the AI a rubric and ask it to grade the learners' responses (see the example in Chapter 11).

- Ask the learners to listen to a lecture and to describe three associations that could help them store the material in memory. Then ask the learners to explain why each association should be effective, and the AI draws on a rubric to grade these explanations.

- Instruct the AI to generate quizzes that require learners to connect concepts and build upon previous learning objectives.

- Ask learners to summarize links between new information and their existing understanding of related topics. The AI provides feedback.

- Have the AI give learners real-world examples or case studies and instruct it to ask the learners to connect these to their existing knowledge and experiences—and the AI then evaluates their responses.

- Ask the AI to develop games and interactive learning activities that require learners to associate new knowledge with enjoyable experiences, thereby increasing engagement and retention.

- Ask learners to generate analogies that relate new concepts to familiar material, and the AI both provides feedback and supplies its own analogies—which the learners evaluate. And the AI, in turn, assesses the quality of those evaluations.

- Instruct the AI to schedule review quizzes that are spaced out over time and that include a different mix of materials. This will help learners form a wider range of associations that later can act as retrieval cues.

—7—

Dual Coding

I s a picture really worth 1,000 words? The answer probably depends on the particular picture and words. Instead of debating how much one modality is worth in another, we are better off thinking about what is gained by combining the modalities. Countless studies have documented that learning is greatly enhanced by combining words and images. This is true for several reasons, but an intriguing one is that different parts of the brain process language and visual information—and areas of the brain that process input often also store that information in a modality-specific long-term memory bank. When learners encounter both words and pictures, their brains have two shots at storing the information, one verbal and one visual.

The Principle of Dual Coding states that *"Learning is more effective when material is presented as both words and images."*[62] Dual Coding gains its force from using two "codes," words and images; images can be visual, auditory, or in any modality. Lectures and active learning are more

---

[62] Kosslyn, S. M. (1994). *Image and brain.* Cambridge, MA: MIT Press; Mayer, R. E. (2001). *Multimedia learning.* NY: Cambridge University Press; Paivio, A. (1971). *Imagery and verbal processes.* New York: Holt, Rinehart, and Winston; Mayer, R. E., & Moreno, R. (2003). Nine ways to reduce cognitive load in multimedia learning. *Educational Psychologist, 38*, 43-52.

effective when they combine words with illustrations, videos, and visual aids.

Showing and Telling

Perhaps the simplest way to draw on this principle during active learning is to ask learners to illustrate and describe the knowledge or skill to be learned. You can ask the learners to employ an AI that produces images to create relevant illustrations, including a sequence of pictures if you've taught learners about an event that unfolds over time. You then ask learners to describe what is depicted, and the combination of images and words should capture the material. Immediately after generating images and descriptions, learners exchange them (e.g., via a Learning Management System) and evaluate how well the images capture what was described—which will lead the learners to process deeply not just their own language-image pairs but also those created by others. This exercise will allow you to leverage a key finding about dual coding: The combined power of words and images is strongest when the two are close to each other, both in time and space.[63]

You can also draw on the Principle of Dual Coding by asking learners to submit an image to an AI that accepts images as input, and prompt the AI to name or describe the object(s) in that image. You can ask the learners to determine whether the AI produces the appropriate name or description. If not, they should create an image that does lead the AI to produce the correct response. You can also have learners ask the AI to provide information about the object(s) in the image, and the learners should then indicate whether this information is appropriate for the fact, concept, idea, event, or skill being illustrated—and if not, they should explain why not. In addition, if the AI is also capable of producing images, you can ask learners to request that the AI produce similar images to what they provide, and the learners should select which image is the best illustration and explain why.

---

[63] Mayer, R. (2009). *Multimedia learning (2nd edition)*. Cambridge, UK: Cambridge University Press.

In short, one way to apply the Principle of Dual Coding is to ask learners to ensure that words and images jointly capture a specific fact, concept, idea, event, or skill.

However, this principle implies more than asking learners to provide or identify the best words and images for specific material. You can also combine visual and verbal material to create something new, which is not conveyed in either modality alone. For example, one way to invoke this principle is to prompt an AI to help create Mind Maps.[64] A Mind Map is a visual way to lay out ideas and indicate how they are related. You can think of a Mind Map by analogy to a hub-and-spokes subway system, where there is a central station, which represents the core knowledge or skills. This central station is connected to smaller stations, which represent related knowledge or skills. And these smaller stations in turn are connected to individual branches that extend to particular destinations, which represent specific knowledge or skills. You can use colors to code the different types of material and also include names and symbols. You can also label the tracks that connect the stations to indicate how knowledge or skills are related.[65]

Figure 7.1 presents an example of a Mind Map that illustrates the concept of a Mind Map.[66]

[64] Farrand, P., Hussain, F., & Hennessy, E. (2002). The efficacy of the mind map study technique. *Medical Education, 36*, 426–431; Nesbit, J.C., & Adesope, O.O. (2006). Learning with concept and knowledge maps: A meta-analysis. *Review of Educational Research, 76*, 413–448.

[65] See, for example, *Mind Map*, https://en.wikipedia.org/wiki/Mind_map; https://www.mindmapping. com

[66] Image by Raphaela Brandner, www.mindmeister.com, reprinted with permission; see https://www. mindmeister.com/blog/why-mind-mapping/

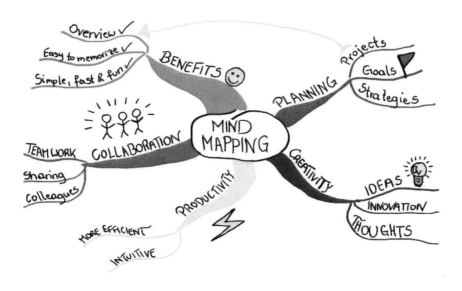

Figure 7.1. *A Mind Map about Mind Maps.*

For example, you can ask learners to use an AI to help create a Mind Map of the five principles presented in this book. You begin by asking each learner to create a Mind Map that illustrates the five principles, their characteristics, and their best applications.[67] The learners should treat AI as an assistant at every step of this process.

1. The learners first enter summaries of the five principles into an AI and then prompt it to indicate what is the central piece of knowledge, which should be placed at the hub. The learners iteratively query the AI until they are satisfied with the results. In this case, the core idea is the science of learning.

---

[67] Respecting the Principle of Chunking, for this Mind Map it would be good to use only two colors for the major branches to form two groups of related principles. For example, you might use red for Deep Processing, Deliberate Practice, and Dual Coding, which are all variants of the general idea "Pay attention and think it through," whereas you might use blue for Chunking and Associations, which are variants of the general idea "Make connections."

2. The learners then ask the AI what the main branches should be, which radiate out from the central hub. The AI might be hit-or-miss, especially on details, so the learners will need to use their judgment when considering the AI's responses. This is a good thing, requiring deep processing. They should decide to have a branch for each of the five principles.

3. After identifying the main branches, the learners repeat the process to identify secondary and tertiary branches. For example, for each of the principles, these sub-branches indicate key characteristics and contexts in which that principle is particularly useful.

4. The learners then employ a software program[68] to create the diagram, with branches for each associated idea, characteristic or context. Some AIs should be able to produce the illustration directly.[69]

5. The learners then ask the AI to describe memorable images to represent each idea and evaluate the candidates until they are satisfied. For example, a picture of a brain might represent the central idea of the science of learning. The learners then produce the corresponding images, evaluate them, and iterate until the images are satisfactory. Finally, in keeping with the Principle of Dual Coding, the learners label each image. It's the combination of words and images that is so powerful. This process is summarized in Figure 7.2.

---

[68] Santos, D. (15 February 2013). *Top 10 totally free mind mapping software tools.* IMDevin: https:// web.archive.org/web/20130807152823/ http://www.imdevin.com/top-10-totally-free-mind- mapping-software-tools/; for paid tools, some of which offer a large range of options, see https://mashable.com/2013/09/25/mind-mapping-tools/

[69] At present, you can have ChatGPT and GPT-4 produce latex code, which you can provide to a service such as Overleaf.com to produce the graphic. In addition, you can use the GPT "Advanced Data Analysis" feature (previously known as "Code Interpreter") to produce many types of graphics directly from GPT. See, for example, Sha, A. (2023, 12 July). How to draw graphs, charts, and diagrams in ChatGPT. *Beebom*, https://beebom.com/how-draw-graphs-charts-diagrams-chatgpt/.

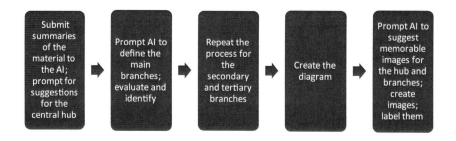

Figure 7.2. *Using AI to help create Mind Maps.*

Using Charts, Graphs, and Diagrams

Mind Maps are a special type of chart, and cannot be used to illustrate all kinds of data or relationships. Generally, an AI can help learners select the best display format if they specify the purpose of the display, the data or a description of the data, and the intended audience.[70]

However, to make the best use of an AI when creating visual displays, learners should be familiar with the different types of visual displays and when each is appropriate. Here's a quick summary.

In general, *charts* organize qualitative information, making clear the relations among the elements. To do so, charts rely on lines or arrows to connect boxes, shapes, pictures of objects, or even just words. Charts are appropriate for illustrating the structure of an object, organization, or event. Depending on what you are teaching, you can ask the AI to deploy appropriate charts in active learning exercises, which will lead learners to utilize both pictures and words when they grasp and take in new information.

For example, my use of flowcharts in this book draws on the Principle of Dual Coding. These illustrations not only complement the text, but also the charts themselves combine graphic elements—the boxes and

---

[70] Learners can also ask the AI to follow principles of display design, such as those summarized in Kosslyn, S. M. (2006). *Graph design for the eye and mind*. New York. Oxford University Press.

arrows—with text. The text and flowcharts give you two ways to grasp and take in the information. I aim to show and tell.

Charts are useful for showing how entities are organized hierarchically. For example, if you are teaching about the structure of an organization, a hierarchical "tree" chart can nicely illustrate who reports to whom. Such a chart is even more memorable if each level is illustrated, and learners can easily have an AI create such illustrations. For instance, you might ask learners to prompt an AI to produce pictures of the uniforms for different ranks in the army.

In contrast, a *diagram* is an abstract picture of an object or situation (e.g., a battle plan or football play). Diagrams typically show just the most important aspects of the object or situation, leaving out the sorts of details about the surface, color, and texture evident in a photograph. Diagrams not only depict parts of the object or situation, they also rely on a combination of symbols (such as arrows), pictures, and words to structure information. If you've ever assembled furniture from Ikea or built a model airplane from a kit, you've probably relied on a diagram to help you assemble it.

Both charts and diagrams illustrate qualitative relationships. *Graphs* are different: they illustrate quantitative relationships. Graphs illustrate the relationships among measured amounts. In all cases, graphs obey the *More is More* rule: The higher or longer the bar, the higher the line, or the larger the wedge in a pie, the more of some quantity is being shown. Learners can enlist AIs to help them select and create specific types of graphs.

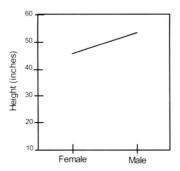

Figure 7.3. *A simple graph shown to undergraduates.*

However, graphs are difficult for many people to interpret and produce. My favorite example, which is by no means an isolated or exceptional case, is a study in which researchers showed Stanford University undergraduates a simple line graph like the one in Figure 7.3. This graph compares the heights of young males and females. When the participants were asked to interpret what they saw, 12% of them claimed that "The more male a person is, the taller he/she is."[71] This was in spite of the fact that in 1999, when this study was published, the prevailing idea about gender was that it is highly binary. Some people find this sort of result difficult to believe and try to explain it in terms of "bad graphs" or the like. For example, in this case, some argue that line graphs should only be shown when there are continuous variations along the X-axis, and thus the participants' assumption of continuous variation makes sense. However, others argue that line graphs should show differences by providing a slope, which thereby relieves the viewer of the effort of imagining a line that connects two bars. In any case, such graphs do appear in various publications, and learners should know how to read them—but they often do not.[72]

---

[71] Zacks, J., & Tversky, B. (1999). Bars and lines: A study of graphic communication. *Memory & Cognition, 27*, 1073–1079.

[72] Zacks & Tversky's finding is not a quirk. For example, see: Delmas, R., Garfield, J., & Ooms, A. (2005). Using assessment items to study students' difficulty reading and interpreting graphical representations of distributions. In K. Makar (Ed.), *Proceedings of*

Thus, you cannot take for granted that learners will know how to interpret charts and graphs. To confirm that learners are equipped to read such displays, ask an AI to conduct a tutorial; to ensure that the tutorial is accurate, submit relevant resources to the AI and ask it to base the tutorial on this material—telling it to use these resources instead of other information it may have. Prompt the AI to assess the learners' comprehension during the tutorial, drilling deeper when learners make mistakes or moving ahead quickly when they clearly know the material.

Visualizing Illustrations

Finally, you can employ the Principle of Dual Coding even without showing a picture: You can prompt an AI to ask learners to "supply their own pictures" by visualizing, creating a mental picture in their "mind's eye." Recall my favorite experiment in cognitive psychology, which I summarized at the beginning of Chapter 4: The researcher presented a series of pairs of words and asked the participants either to verbalize the words silently or to visualize the named objects interacting in some way (e.g., for the pair "cow-tree" they might visualize a cow rubbing against a tree). When the participants' memories were tested later, the researcher found that visualizing objects resulted in about twice as many word pairs being recalled as were recalled after only verbalizing them. In Chapter 4, I emphasized that this finding reflects the amount of deep mental processing that was required to do the two tasks. In Chapter 4, we also

---

the fourth international research forum on statistical reasoning, literacy, and reasoning. Auckland, NZ: University of Auckland; Friel, S. N., Curcio, F., & Bright, G. W. (2001). Making sense of graphs: Critical factors influencing comprehension and instructional implications. *Journal for Research in Mathematics Education, 32,* 124-158; Glazer, N. (2011). Challenges with graph interpretation: a review of the literature. *Studies in Science Education, 47,* 183-210; Shah, P. (2002). Graph comprehension: The role of format, content, and individual difference. In M. Anderson, B. Mayer & P. Olivier (Eds.), *Diagrammatic representation and reasoning* (pp. 207–222). London & New York: Springer Verlag; Shah, P., & Carpenter, P.A. (1995). Conceptual limitations in comprehending line graphs. *Journal of Experimental Psychology, 124,* 43–61; Shah, P., & Hoeffner, J. (2002). Review of graph comprehension research: Implications for instruction. *Educational Psychology Review, 14,* 47–69; McDermott, L.C., Rosenquist, M.L., & van Zee, E.H. (1987). Student difficulties in connecting graphs and physics: Examples from kinematics. *American Journal of Physics, 55,* 503–513.

saw that what learners remember depends on which information is processed deeply (for example, about sounds versus meaning). What I didn't mention previously is that an activity can lead learners to deeply process more than a single type of information about the material, which enhances learning even more. To create mental images in that experiment, the participants needed to process both the names, to understand them and dig out the corresponding visual memory, and the previously stored visual information itself. In so doing, they were creating two kinds of new memories of the pair: One verbal, the names themselves, and one visual, how the named objects "appeared" in the mental image they created. Deeply processing both sorts of information vastly improved their memories. Evidence indicates that people often spontaneously visualize named objects (e.g., "car," "table," "doorknob"), which makes them more memorable than abstract concepts (e.g., "truth," "justice," "integrity").[73]

You can prompt an AI to lead learners to visualize specific material. For example, the activity shown in Box 12 should help learners achieve the learning objective "Identify key events in the founding of Nigeria." You can easily adapt this activity to address many learning objectives. Here are the instructions sent to the learners:

Instruction to the Learner
You will soon see a story about the founding of the west-African country Nigeria. Visualize the events as they are described. At specific points, the AI will pause and ask you to describe the mental images you just formed; at that point, type in a brief description. The AI will provide feedback on your images.

You would send learners those instructions along with the following prompt, which the learners should submit to an AI:

---

[73] Paivio, A. (1971). *Imagery and verbal processes*. New York: Holt, Rinehart, and Winston.

AI Prompt

I want you to tell an accurate story about the founding of the west-African country Nigeria. Instruct the user that they are to visualize the events as you describe them. After you have described an event that is easy to visualize, stop and ask the learner to describe the mental images they just formed. Do not provide the answer, but instead, wait for the learner to type in their description of the image they formed. After the learner is finished typing, provide feedback on these images, indicating whether they were appropriate and how they could be improved. Following this, continue the story, being sure to touch on key elements of the history, asking about the mental images, and providing feedback.

Box 12 presents how the AI responded to that prompt. As you can see, it did a nice job of inducing relevant mental images and managed to make the material remarkably vivid.

BOX 12: Using AI to induce mental images in learners

AI:
Great, let's start our journey.

Imagine yourself in the year 1861, in a time of discovery, exploration, and colonial conquest. Picture yourself standing on the edge of a vast river that is teeming with life. The water is the color of dark chocolate, mirroring the rich brown of the earth that lines its banks. This is the mighty Niger River, the lifeline of West Africa, and it's here, in the bustling port city of Lagos, that our story begins.

The air is thick with the smell of saltwater, fish, and spices, the sounds of haggling voices fill the air as people bustle around, their clothes a vibrant mix of colors. In the distance, you can see the tall masts of a European ship just arriving. This ship represents the British Empire, and its presence marks the beginning of a significant shift in the balance of power in the region. Lagos, once a thriving independent city-state, is about to be annexed by the British.

Now, pause for a moment and form a mental image of this scene. What does it look like? What are the colors, sounds, and smells? Take your time and type your visualization when you're ready.

Me:
I see a seaport full of energetic people who are haggling and trading various sorts of goods, ranging from food to jewelry.

AI:
Your visualization is on point. The bustling energy of the seaport and the variety of goods being traded reflect the vibrant economy and culture of Lagos at that time. Now, imagine not just the physical items, but also the atmosphere. The voices overlapping in different languages, the smell of food, spices, and the sea, the heat of the tropical sun. The scene is not just about activity, but also the rich sensory experience of being in a busy port city.

Let's move on in our story.

The British Empire, under the guise of ending the slave trade, slowly began to establish control over other parts of what we now know as Nigeria. Picture the year 1885, the Berlin Conference where Africa was divided among the European powers with no African input. The territory that would become Nigeria was ceded to the British.

Now, let's fast forward to the early 20th century. The British had consolidated their control over the region, amalgamating the Northern and Southern Protectorates into a single entity known as the Colony and Protectorate of Nigeria in 1914. Picture an administrative office, filled with British officials drawing lines on maps, reshaping the destiny of millions of people.

What images does this new chapter evoke for you? Take a moment to picture it.

Me:
I visualize an aristocratic man sitting at a table with representatives of the tribes. He has paper and pen in front of him, and has served the tribe members tea.

AI:
Your image captures the diplomatic setting where such decisions might have been made, but it's important to remember that the amalgamation process was a unilateral decision by the British, with little to no input from the local tribal leaders. The scene you're picturing might be more applicable to later periods of negotiation for independence.

Try to imagine instead a room filled with British officials, far away from Nigeria, in a room filled with maps, charts, and documents. There is likely a heavy feeling of responsibility, but also a sense of entitlement and disregard for the complex tribal, cultural, and linguistic landscapes they are tampering with. They are deciding the fate of a land and people they barely understand, marking territories with a ruler and a pen.
Now let's move to the next phase of Nigeria's history.

By the mid-20th century, the winds of change were blowing across Africa. Imagine the year 1960, Nigeria is on the cusp of a new era. The green-white-green flag of Nigeria flutters in the wind for the first time as the country celebrates its independence on October 1st. The crowds are jubilant, their faces illuminated by the glow of fireworks against the night sky.

Take a moment to visualize this scene. What does it look like? What are the emotions that you can perceive?

Me:
I see Model-T cars on the street honking their horns and people dancing in the street, waving flags.

AI:
Great! Your visualization captures the excitement and joy of that historic moment. The scene is full of movement, with cars honking and people dancing, which perfectly reflects the atmosphere of celebration. However, remember that by 1960, more modern cars would have been in use, not the Model-T, which was prevalent in the early 20th century. Try to imagine more contemporary vehicles for that era and perhaps add more details like the sound of music, the explosion of fireworks, and the vibrant colors of traditional attire mixed with western style clothing. The joy on people's faces, the hope in their eyes for a brighter future, these are all parts of this momentous scene.

Now, let's continue to the next part of the story.

After gaining independence, Nigeria was a country of great promise, but also significant challenges. It was home to a rich diversity of ethnic groups, each with its own language, culture, and traditions. This diversity was both a strength and a source of tension.

Now, it's the year 1967. The air is thick with tension and the mood is heavy. The Eastern region of Nigeria, predominantly Igbo, has declared itself the independent Republic of Biafra, sparking a bloody civil war that would last for three years. Picture yourself on a hill overlooking a battlefield. The ground is scarred by the marks of conflict, the air is filled with the acrid smell of gunpowder and the sounds of distant gunfire. Take a moment to visualize this scene. What does it look like? What are the emotions that you can perceive?

Me:
I'm at a loss. How can I visualize such a thing?

AI:
It's completely understandable if you're finding it difficult to visualize such a tragic and complex event. War scenes are indeed tough to picture. In such instances, it might be more helpful to focus on the broader implications or the emotions associated with such moments. Imagine the confusion and fear among ordinary people, the chaos of families having to flee their homes, the sorrow of communities torn apart. Picture the resilience of the human spirit in times of adversity. Visualize the profound sense of uncertainty that would have marked this period, but also the determination to survive and hope for a better future.

Remember, the objective of this exercise is not to delve into the horrors of war, but to understand the gravity of the situation and the drastic change it represented in Nigeria's history. Let's continue our story from here.

The civil war finally ended in 1970, but its effects lingered. Despite the difficulties, Nigeria persevered. The country gradually transitioned from military rule to democratic governance.

Fast forward to May 29, 1999, a momentous day in Nigeria's history. Picture the inauguration of Olusegun Obasanjo, a former military head of state who had now been democratically elected as president. The crowd is a sea of color, people waving Nigerian flags with hope and apprehension. There's a sense of cautious optimism in the air.

Imagine the scene - the crowd, the anticipation, the solemnity of the oath-taking ceremony. What does it look like? What are the emotions that you can perceive?

Me:
Some people are standing silently at the ceremony, others are chattering excitedly, and the crowd is very dense, jostling against each other. There is a sense of anticipation, hope, and happiness in the air.

AI:
Excellent visualization! You've managed to capture the varied emotions of the crowd - the excitement, hope, and nervous anticipation of this historic moment. The density of the crowd also reflects the significance of the event and the high public interest. Remember to imagine the colors of the Nigerian flags being waved in the crowd, the formal attire of the officials, and the sound of the national anthem being played.
In conclusion, Nigeria's history is a complex tapestry of diverse cultures, colonial rule, struggle for independence, civil war, and the eventual transition to democracy. By visualizing these events, you can better understand and appreciate the journey of this resilient nation.

Remember, visualization is a powerful tool for learning and understanding. It makes abstract concepts tangible and enhances memory and recall. Keep practicing, and you'll find it gets easier with time.

In short, active learning exercises should take advantage of the Principle of Dual Coding whenever it is appropriate, given the content and learning objective. The activity should lead learners to create or otherwise pay attention to, and rely on, both perceptual and verbal information. The key is simply to show and tell—or induce learners to show and tell (even if the "showing" is entirely in their mind's eye). AI can help learners engage in these activities.

Using AI to Develop Activities

You can use AI to create active learning exercises that invoke the Principle of Dual Coding by submitting the following prompt. You again need to adapt the prompt so that the "objective" for the AI grows out of your learning objective and you need to specify the level of the learners.

AI Prompt

Objective: Engage in a real-time, active learning exchange with a human learner about the structure of the US federal government. Guidelines: Interactive Dialogue: Engage in a one-on-one dialogue with the learner. Ask one question at a time and always wait for the learner's response before proceeding. Solo Activity: Ensure all interactions are only between the learner and GPT-4, or role-played entities introduced by GPT-4. Engagement Level: Make the activity engaging, fun, and novel. Focus on one learning principle: Rely on the Active Learning Principle of Dual Coding, which states: "Learning is more effective when material is both shown and described—and when learners are led to illustrate what they have learned; this principle implies that appropriate illustrations—including charts and graphs—should be included when they can usefully supplement descriptions." People can also "illustrate" to themselves, using mental images. Example: Using an infographic along with a descriptive paragraph or visualizing a complex scene. Target Audience: Keep the activity at a university level. Do Not Reference Dual Coding Principle: Avoid mentioning the Active Learning Principle of Dual Coding. Begin the activity when ready.

Box 13 shows what I got from GPT-4 when I put in that prompt:

Box 13: An example of how AI can employ the Principle of Dual Coding

AI:
Great! Let's embark on an exploration of the structure of the U.S. federal government. As you may know, it's divided into three branches: the Legislative, the Executive, and the Judicial.

Let's start with a little activity. Can you visualize the U.S. Capitol building? This is where the legislative branch of the U.S. government meets. Picture the grand, white building with its iconic dome and the House of Representatives and Senate chambers on either side.

Can you name the two chambers that comprise the legislative branch?

Me:
House of Representatives and Senate

AI:
Excellent! You're absolutely right. The U.S. Capitol building is home to both the House of Representatives and the Senate.

Now, let's imagine a scale. On one side, we have the House of Representatives. The number of representatives each state has is proportional to its population - the more populous the state, the more representatives it has.

On the other side, we have the Senate. Here, every state, regardless of its size or population, is represented equally. Each state has two senators.

Now, can you tell me what the term lengths are for members of each chamber?

Me:
Six years for Senate, two years for House

AI:

Correct! Senators serve six-year terms and Representatives serve two-year terms.

Now, let's move on to the Executive branch. Picture the White House, an iconic symbol of this branch. The executive branch is headed by the President, who is aided by the Vice President and the Cabinet.

With that in mind, can you tell me who makes up the Cabinet, and how are they chosen?

Me:
The President selects Cabinet members, who chair and run major departments of the Executive Branch

AI:
That's correct! The President appoints the members of the Cabinet, who each lead a major department of the federal government. These appointments are subject to confirmation by the Senate.

Now, let's visualize the third branch: The Judicial branch. Picture the Supreme Court building, a grand structure with massive columns in the front. The Supreme Court is the highest court in the U.S. and it's here that the most consequential legal decisions are made.

The Supreme Court consists of nine justices. Do you know how these justices are appointed, and for how long they serve?

Me:
The President nominates, Senate confirms, and they are appointed for life

AI:
Correct! Supreme Court Justices are nominated by the President and confirmed by the Senate. Once appointed, they serve for life or until they choose to retire.

To recap: We have the legislative branch with the Senate and the House of Representatives meeting in the Capitol. We have the executive branch, with the President, Vice President, and the Cabinet operating from the White House. Finally, we have the judicial branch, symbolized by the Supreme Court, with justices serving for life.

This trinity of separation of powers, checks and balances is a cornerstone of the U.S. federal government.

Now, for a bit more of a challenge: Can you describe one way each of these branches can check or limit the power of the others?

Me:
The Legislature can: 1) impeach the President (Executive Branch) and 2) override judicial rulings (if the laws are constitutional). The Judiciary can: 1) adjudicate elections for President (Executive Branch) and 2) rule that laws passed by the Legislative Branch are unconstitutional. The Executive Branch can: 1) issue Executive Orders to circumvent the Legislature, and 2) expand the size of the Supreme Court to "pack the court" (in theory... but this is not a good idea).

AI:
Excellent! You've accurately identified ways in which each branch of the U.S. government can check or limit the power of the others.

The checks and balances system is indeed a critical part of the U.S. federal structure. It helps to ensure that no single branch becomes too powerful and that the government operates in the best interests of its citizens.

Our visual journey has taken us from the Capitol building, to the White House, and finally to the Supreme Court. Along the way, we've met the key players and understood the critical role each branch plays.

To wrap up our session, can you summarize in your own words the structure of the U.S. federal government and the principle of checks and balances?

Me:
The US Government has three branches, Executive, Legislative and Judicial, and each has its own domain of power. However, each branch can -- at least to some extent -- curtail, shape or respond to the other branches.

AI:
Exactly! The U.S. federal government is a complex system designed with a separation of powers and checks and balances. This structure ensures that no single branch becomes too powerful. The three branches—Executive, Legislative, and Judicial—each have their own responsibilities, but they also have the ability to influence and check the actions of the other branches.

By visualizing the iconic buildings associated with each branch, we can better remember and understand the separate but interconnected roles they play. Your understanding and ability to summarize these concepts demonstrates a good grasp of the U.S. government's structure. Well done!

Are there any other aspects of the U.S. federal government you'd like to explore further?

Me:
No thank you.

AI:
You're welcome! I'm glad I could assist you in understanding the structure of the U.S. federal government. If you have any more questions in the future, don't hesitate to ask. Happy learning!

This exercise did not exploit the Principle of Dual Coding well because it did not combine descriptions and images very effectively. We can improve the prompt to lead the AI to integrate the descriptions and imagery. Moreover, we can encourage the learners to use imagery by instructing the AI to ask occasional questions about the mental images that the learners should create. For example, the AI could ask learners to judge which of two named buildings is taller, which typically requires imagery.[74] We can easily iterate on the prompt to induce the AI to include

---

[74] Kosslyn, S.M. (1980). *Image and mind.* Cambridge, MA: Harvard University Press.

such techniques to encourage the learners to create mental images that complement the verbal descriptions.

Here are some additional examples of particular types of exercises that draw on the Principle of Dual Coding. In each case, you can give the AI a rubric and ask it to evaluate the learners' responses (see the example in Chapter 11).

- Use an AI to generate a series of illustrations for a given description. Following this, ask the learners to evaluate the illustrations and rank them in terms of appropriateness for the description, explaining the criteria they developed.

- Provide a dozen images and descriptions to an AI that accepts images and ask it to match the descriptions to the images and to explain why those matches make sense. Following this, ask learners to evaluate the responses.

- Provide two images and two descriptions to an AI that accepts images and ask it to match the descriptions to the images. Ask the learners then to make the descriptions increasingly ambiguous until the AI has difficulty. The learners then explain why the modifications disrupted the AI from finding the appropriate relation between the visual and verbal.

- Ask learners to prompt an AI to design a game that involves visualizing named materials in order to learn them. After receiving the response, the learners start a new chat and ask the AI to evaluate this game and to improve it. The learners repeat this process until they think the game would be very effective, and then try it out on a friend or colleague.

- Ask learners to submit a data set to an AI that has the equivalent of the Advanced Data Analysis feature of GPT-4, and prompt it to generate the most appropriate graphic. Learners evaluate the results and then ask the AI to modify the graphic so that it is appropriate for grade-school children and evaluate whether the AI is successful—and explain why or why not.

—8—

Deliberate Practice

After accepting a job to work in France for a year, I was keen to learn to speak the language. I soon realized that I was not good at noticing the nuances of what I heard and had trouble pronouncing French words. Thus, I found a native speaker who was willing to work as a tutor. It turned out that I was able to overcome (largely) this issue by using a simple technique: I tried to say a word or phrase in French, and my tutor then repeated it back with the proper accent. I listened very carefully and said it again, trying to reduce the difference between what I had said initially and what she had then said. We typically repeated this process several times with the same word. Although often slightly frustrating, my pronunciation did get better and I was (largely) understandable once I finally arrived at my new job.

This way of learning makes use of the Principle of Deliberate Practice, which states that "*Learning is enhanced by using feedback to focus on practicing the most challenging aspects of a task.*" The key idea here is that to learn effectively, learners shouldn't just repeat something over and over. This is mindless practice. Instead, learners should identify rough patches and zero in on them, devoting disproportionate time and effort to mastering the aspects that are most challenging for them.[75]

Critically, learners need to rely on feedback to identify the most challenging aspects of acquiring specific information or a skill. Such feedback should address a well-defined behavior, be concrete, and be provided as soon as possible after the behavior. The feedback should help the learners to identify exactly what they need to improve and should indicate how to improve it.[76] Just saying "pretty good" is not effective because this doesn't tell the learners which aspects of what they did were good and which aspects need work. (This reminds me of a story I heard about the filming of one of the early Star Wars movies: After a take, the director told the cast "Do it again, only better." They did not find this very helpful.) Crucially, the feedback should not address a learner's failings as a human being but instead should focus on what they need to do to improve.

Deliberate Practice, Step-by-Step

The steps of deliberate practice are outlined in Figure 8.1.

1. As shown, the first thing a learner needs to do is to demonstrate how well they have already attained the learning objective. In my French example, I demonstrated what I had, and had not, learned by trying to say a French word or phrase. This principle applies to all aspects of knowledge or skills that learners can demonstrate, ranging from a golf swing, to writing computer code, to giving a speech. With the advent of video input, you can even use

---

[75] Brown, P. C., Roediger, H. L. III, and McDaniel, M. A. (2014). *Make it stick: The science of successful learning*. New York: Belknap Press; Ericsson, K. A., Krampe, R. T., & Tesch-Romer, C. (1993). The role of deliberate practice in the acquisition of expert performance. *Psychological Review, 100,* 363-406.

[76] Hattie, J., & Timperley, H. (2007). The power of feedback. *Review of Educational Research, 77,* 81-112; Kluger, A. N., & DeNisi, A. (1998). Feedback interventions: Toward the understanding of a double-edged sword. *Current Directions in Psychological Science, 7,* 67–72.

AIs to evaluate how well you play sports and similar activities that require large-scale physical interactions with objects or other people.

2. The next step is to receive feedback, which typically includes an example of the correct, or clearly better, version of what the learner tried to do—a native speaker saying the word, an expert coach demonstrating the golf swing, and so forth. The feedback needs to emphasize the specific aspects that the learner needs to improve. For example, my French teacher might have focused on the "r" sound that I was making incorrectly, perhaps even exaggerating it so that its distinctive features were clearly evident.

3. Crucially, the learner needs to pay close attention to the correct behavior and notice the disparity between what they did and what they should have done.

4. The learner needs to use that observation to update how they think about what they should do—which will affect their performance in the future.

5. Finally, the learner should repeat the behavior, observe whether it is closer to the model, and repeat Steps 2 - 5 as needed until the behavior is satisfactory.

Deliberate practice requires learners to pay close attention at every step of the way and make a deliberate effort to reconceive what they are doing. This is difficult: Learners need to keep in mind their initial try, the feedback, what's different between their initial try and the feedback, and then they need to adjust their next attempt.[77]

---

[77] cf. Ericsson, K. A., Prietula, M. J., & Cokely, E. T. (2007, July-August). The making of an expert. *Harvard Business Review*: https://hbr.org/2007/07/the-making-of-an-expert

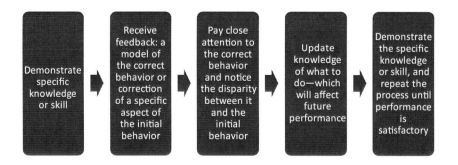

Figure 8.1. *Steps of deliberate practice.*

Learners need to venture outside their comfort zone to get the most out of deliberate practice—they need to push themselves to do something they find difficult and persist in trying, and trying again, to improve. In deliberate practice, learners focus mainly—or only—on the parts that they need to improve. This can be frustrating because they are continually falling short as they learn. In my French example, I didn't repeat words that I already pronounced clearly enough, I only focused on the words I had difficulty with—which was a bit demoralizing. In fact, deliberate practice requires learners to make errors, which they rely on to identify where they need to improve.[78] The power of "productive failures" is well documented, particularly in the context of problem solving. In this case, learners explore different ways of solving a problem and discover which avenues don't work.[79] However, deliberate practice is not effective if learners reach too

---

[78] Mayer, R. E. (2008). *Learning and instruction*. Upper Saddle River, New Jersey: Pearson Education, Inc.

[79] Kapur, M. (2016). Examining productive failure, productive success, unproductive failure, and unproductive success in learning. *Educational Psychologist, 51*, 289–299. https://doi.org/10.1080/00461520.2016.1155457; Kapur, M. (2008). Productive failure. *Cognition and Instruction, 26*, 379–424. doi: 10.1080/ 07370000802212669; Sinha, T., & Kapur, M. (2021). Robust effects of the efficacy of explicit failure-driven scaffolding in problem-solving prior to instruction: A replication and extension. *Learning and Instruction, 75*: 101488. doi: 10.1016/j.learninstruc.2021.101488; Sinha, T., Kapur, M., West, R., Catasta, M., Hauswirth, M., & Trninic, D. (2021). Differential benefits of explicit failure-driven and success-driven scaffolding in problem-solving prior to instruction. *Journal of Educational Psychology, 113*, 530–555. doi: 10.1037/edu0000483.

far outside their comfort zone. Again, the new material must not be so easy that it's boring or so difficult that it's frustrating—you need to aim for the "Goldilocks spot."[80]

An AI can easily help learners engage in deliberate practice. For example, let's say that the learner has received feedback that they are not using metaphors and similes appropriately, and they realize that they don't really understand the difference. An AI can help them learn this distinction easily using the following prompt:

AI Prompt

Please write a six-sentence paragraph about Paris, France, that uses many similes and metaphors. Present the sentences one at a time; stop at the end of each sentence where a simile or metaphor was used. At that point, ask the user to choose: "simile" or "metaphor." If the user gets it wrong, correct them and provide the explanation. Continue this process until the paragraph is finished.

Box 14 presents how the AI responded. As you can see, it did a nice job of providing feedback where it was needed.

BOX 14: Using AI to teach the distinction between metaphors and similes

AI:
Paris, like a beautifully bound book, holds a wealth of stories within its cover. Is this a simile or a metaphor?

Me:
simile

---

[80] For a more general statement of the utility of pushing students a bit beyond their comfort zones, see Bjork, E. L., & Bjork, R. A. (2011). Making things hard on yourself, but in a good way: Creating desirable difficulties to enhance learning. In M. A. Gernsbacher, R. W. Pew, L. M. Hough, J. R. Pomerantz, & FABBS Foundation (Eds.), *Psychology and the real world: Essays illustrating fundamental contributions to society* (p. 56–64). New York: Worth Publishers.

AI:
Correct! It's a simile because the sentence uses the word "like" to compare Paris to a beautifully bound book. Let's move on to the next sentence.

Its streets are veins, pulsing with the lifeblood of culture and history. Is this a simile or a metaphor?

Me:
simile

AI:
Actually, this is a metaphor. The sentence compares Paris's streets to veins without using "like" or "as", which is the defining characteristic of a metaphor. It directly states that the streets are veins, implying they are vital pathways filled with culture and history, much like veins carry blood, the life sustainer in our bodies. Let's move to the next sentence.
The Eiffel Tower, standing tall and proud, is like a lighthouse guiding lost souls home. Is this a simile or a metaphor?

Me:
simile

AI:
Correct! It's a simile because it uses the word "like" to compare the Eiffel Tower to a lighthouse. Now let's continue.
The hustle and bustle of the city is the symphony of urban life, with each arrondissement playing its own unique note. Is this a simile or a metaphor?

Me:
metaphor

AI:
Correct! It's a metaphor because it equates the hustle and bustle of the city to a symphony, without using the words "like" or "as". Let's move on to the next sentence.

The River Seine snakes through the city like a ribbon of liquid history. Is this a simile or a metaphor?

> **Me:**
> metaphor
>
> **AI:**
> Actually, this is a simile. The sentence uses the word "like" to compare the River Seine to a ribbon of liquid history. A simile is a figure of speech that directly compares two things using words such as "like" or "as". Let's move on to the final sentence.
>
> Paris, a glittering gem amidst the European continent, holds its charm eternal. Is this a simile or a metaphor?
>
> **Me:**
> metaphor
>
> Correct! It's a metaphor because it refers to Paris as a "glittering gem," directly comparing it without using the words "like" or "as". Well done! We've now finished our six-sentence paragraph about Paris with a mixture of similes and metaphor.

An important point made by this example is that deliberate practice is not just for skills, such as those drawn on when you speak a language or play a musical instrument. Deliberate practice can help people learn anything that they can express, such as the use of different types of words. If you can express it, you can receive feedback about misconceptions and knowledge gaps, which allows you to identify where you need to focus on improving.

Selective Attention

To employ deliberate practice effectively, learners must pay attention to the relevant aspects of what they are trying to learn. For example, ear training requires paying attention to the pitch (the musical note, such as C versus E) and not the timbre (the "color" or "texture" of a note—as illustrated by the difference between the same note being played on a piano versus a flute). Another example: When I was learning French pronunciation, I learned that I needed to pay attention to the purity of vowels.

Interleaving (i.e., mixing up) can lead learners to pay attention to the appropriate aspect of what they are learning. Researchers have found that interleaving different types of instances from the same general category is often a better way to learn than *blocking* together the same types of instances.[81] For example, if the goal is to teach people to identify paintings by specific artists, it's better to ask them to study paintings by different artists (e.g., Monet, Seurat, and Signac) that are interleaved than to study each artist's work one at a time. Of note, when asked afterward, participants believed that intermixing the artists was less effective than studying them one at a time—which is the opposite of what the researchers actually found, and again should make us cautious about accepting our intuitions about how people learn best. Mixing up the examples leads learners to compare and contrast them, which helps them to learn the distinctive characteristics of each artist's style. [82] By interleaving, you lead learners to recognize what they need to focus on when they then engage in deliberate practice. Clearly, you can use an AI to create study sessions that are interleaved and you can instruct it to present the material in a different order for each study session, which should enhance the effect by requiring learners to pay close attention.

However, a word of caution: Interleaving is better than blocking only after learners know enough about each of the to-be-learned categories to make the necessary distinctions. For example, studies have shown that when first learning to pronounce words in a foreign language, learners do better when they learn words with the same pronunciation blocked together rather than being intermixed with words that have different

---

[81] Pan, S. C. (2015, Aug 4). The interleaving effect: Mixing it up boosts learning. *Scientific American:* https://www.scientificamerican.com/article/the-interleaving-effect-mixing-it-up-boosts-learning/; Rohrer, D. (2012). Interleaving helps students distinguish among similar concepts. *Educational Psychology Review, 24,* 355–367.

[82] Kornell, N., & Bjork, R. A. (2008). Learning concepts and categories: Is spacing the "enemy of induction"? *Psychological Science, 19,* 585-592.

pronunciations.[83] When just getting off the ground, the main problem is to get the basic idea of how the novel vowels and consonants sound, which is a prerequisite for making distinctions among them. If learners have no idea what to pay attention to in order to distinguish among categories, mixing up different types of examples may be confusing. AI can help here: You can prompt an AI first to test a learner to determine their level of familiarity with the materials, and then to draw on that information to automatically provide blocked or mixed orders, depending on the level of familiarity.

Interleaving can function as a special case of a more general technique, which simply requires learners to make comparisons and contrasts. The key is to provide learners with a model of what should be learned and to contrast it with specific examples—which ideally differ from the model in only a single way. By leading the learners to notice the differences between the model and the examples, learners can identify what to pay attention to when refining their knowledge and behavior.[84] For instance, if you wanted learners to pronounce Spanish words properly, you might have them listen to a series of words that were pronounced correctly or incorrectly, and they would need to identify which was which. The trick here is to have the incorrect words differ in a minimal way from the correct ones. This procedure will sensitize learners to the sounds that they should produce. Going back to teaching the styles of different artists, you could pair a genuine example with a fabricated version that differs in a subtle way, and learners have to pick out which is which—and receive feedback, which directs them to pay attention to distinctive characteristics. In fact, an art museum actually did this, displaying originals that were paired with forgeries![85]

---

[83] Carpenter, S. K., & Mueller, F. E. (2013). The effects of interleaving versus blocking on foreign language pronunciation learning. *Memory & Cognition, 41,* 671-682.

[84] Bransford, J. D., & McCarrel, N. S. (1974). A sketch of a cognitive approach to comprehension. In W. Weimer & D. S. Palermo (Ed.), *Cognition and the symbolic processes.* (pp. 189-229). Hillsdale, NJ: Erlbaum Associates.

[85] As described in Gardner, H. (1982). *Art, mind, and brain: A cognitive approach to creativity.* New York: Basic Books.

Shaping is another technique that can help learners identify what to pay attention to when they engage in deliberate practice.[86] Shaping occurs when you start with a very broad distinction, provide feedback until learners master it, and then narrow down the distinction, repeating the process until you reach the appropriate level of precision. For example, when conducting ear training, an instructor may initially simply want learners to distinguish between notes that are higher versus lower in pitch. The instructor might start with notes that are separated by an octave, which is very easy, and then go to a fifth, which is closer in pitch, and then to a third, and then to a second and finally a semitone. You can easily deploy an AI to deliver many types of shaping.

Deliberate Practice at Scale

Until the advent of AI, deliberate practice was difficult to implement at scale. The traditional way to help learners engage in deliberate practice is to have a human tutor work directly with each individual learner. This is what my French tutor did, what golf coaches do, what expert surgeons training medical residents do. However, this sort of individualized tutoring is expensive and gifted tutors may be hard to find. AI provides an inexpensive way to do this for many applications. For example, Box 15 shows how I used GPT-4 as a writing tutor. As you can see, it can clearly help learners address issues about grammar (material in brackets was added later for clarity).

BOX 15: Using AI as a writing tutor

Me:
Correct the grammatical errors in the following and summarize your corrections and the reasons for your corrections at the end:

Birdwatching, a fascinating and relaxing hobby, allows people to connect with nature and learn about the diverse species inhabiting our world. By

---

[86] See Kosslyn, S. M., & Rosenberg, R. S. (2020). *Introducing psychology: Brain, person, group (5th edition)*. Boston, MA: FlatWorld.

observing birds in their natural habitats, birdwatchers gains a deeper appreciation for the intricate ecosystems these creatures are part of. Not only do it heighten environmental awareness, but also provides opportunities for socializing with like-minded individuals and discovering new, rare birds, making birdwatching a truly rewarding and enjoyable pursuit.

AI:
Birdwatching, a fascinating and relaxing hobby, allows people to connect with nature and learn about the diverse species inhabiting our world. By observing birds in their natural habitats, birdwatchers gain a deeper appreciation for the intricate ecosystems these creatures are part of. Not only does it heighten environmental awareness, but it also provides opportunities for socializing with like-minded individuals and discovering new, rare birds, making birdwatching a truly rewarding and enjoyable pursuit.

Summary of corrections and reasons:
1. Changed "birdwatchers gains" to "birdwatchers gain" because the subject "birdwatchers" is plural and should be followed by the plural verb form "gain."
2. Changed "do it heighten" to "does it heighten" to correct the subject-verb agreement. The subject "it" (referring to birdwatching) is singular, so it should be followed by the singular verb form "does."
3. Changed "but also provides" to "but it also provides" to maintain parallelism and ensure a clear subject for the verb "provides." The subject "it" (referring to birdwatching) should be included in the second part of the compound sentence to match the structure of the first part.

[This led me to add a new prompt, which builds on the previous one:]

Me:
Thank you! Now, please give me exercises where you ask me to correct instances of these kinds of errors, engaging me in "deliberate practice."

AI:
Certainly! Here are five sentences with errors related to subject-verb agreement and parallelism. Correct the errors in each sentence, and I'll provide feedback on your corrections.

1. Dogs enjoys playing fetch, and cats loves to chase laser pointers.
2. Running in the park not only strengthens your muscles but also improving your cardiovascular health.
4. Students needs to submit their homework before class, while teachers has to grade them after class.
5. The sun set, the stars appear, and the night becomes darker.
6. The new supermarket offers fresh produce, a wide range of products, and have a friendly staff.

After you provide your corrected sentences, I'll give you feedback and explain the reasons for the corrections.

Me:
1. Dogs enjoy playing fetch, and cats love to chase laser pointers.
2. Running in the park not only strengthens your muscles but also improves your cardiovascular health.
3. Students need to submit their homeworks before class, while teachers must grade them after class.
4. The sun sets, the stars appears, and the night becomes darker.
5. The new supermarket offers fresh produce, a wide range of products, and has a friendly staff.

AI:
Great job! You've successfully corrected most of the errors. Here's the feedback on your corrections:

1. Correct. You've fixed the subject-verb agreement by changing "enjoys" to "enjoy" and "loves" to "love" for the plural subjects "dogs" and "cats."
2. Correct. You've fixed the parallelism issue by changing "improving" to "improves," making both parts of the sentence consistent.
3. Almost correct. You've fixed the subject-verb agreement by changing "needs" to "need" and "has" to "must." However, the word "homework" is an uncountable noun, so it should remain as "homework," not "homeworks."
4. Almost correct. You've fixed the subject-verb agreement by changing "set" to "sets." However, you should change "appears" to "appear" to agree with the plural subject "stars."

6. Almost correct. You've addressed the parallelism issue by adding "has" before "a friendly staff." However, to make the sentence fully parallel, you can rephrase it as: "The new supermarket offers fresh produce, a wide range of products, and a friendly staff."

Revised sentences:
3. Students need to submit their homework before class, while teachers must grade them after class.
4. The sun sets, the stars appear, and the night becomes darker.
5. The new supermarket offers fresh produce, a wide range of products, and a friendly staff.

GPT-4 "knows" what deliberate practice is and can employ it effectively. Indeed, using AI to provide deliberate practice solves another part of the problem of relying on human tutors to provide deliberate practice. Namely, experts often are not good at teaching their field because their expertise has led them to forget what is difficult for novices. To give high-quality feedback, the tutor needs to understand the sorts of errors that an expert no longer makes. And the problem is worse than that: The process of becoming an expert involves converting a lot of declarative knowledge to automatic, unconscious procedural knowledge (see Chapter 3)—and thus experts may not even be aware of how they actually perform tasks in their field of expertise. As a familiar example, if you can ride a bike, you probably are not aware of how you balance on it—you just "do it." In fact, studies have shown that "when experts in many different subject-matter areas teach or train, they leave out approximately 70 percent of the knowledge required to perform adequately." [87] Such incomplete instruction prevents learners from mastering the material.[88] AI can clearly help.

---

[87] Clark, R. E. (2011). The impact of non-conscious knowledge on educational technology research and design. *Educational Technology, July-August*, 3-11, p. 4.

[88] Clark, R. E., Yates, K., Early, S., & Moulton, K. (2010). An analysis of the failure of electronic media and discovery-based learning: Evidence for the performance benefits of guided training methods. In K. H. Silber & W. R. Foshay (Eds.), *Handbook of improving*

We can extend the reach of AIs by using a method that does not involve having it correct the user. Crucially, this sort of feedback does not require a tutor. Such deliberate practice relies on a standard or model that learners can use for feedback. For example, Benjamin Franklin learned to write well by studying an article he found particularly well written, and then a few days later, he would write it down in his own words. He then compared his version with the original and noted the differences between the two, focusing on where he had fallen short. Following this, he worked on improving those particular characteristics of his own writing, and then repeated the process with another article. Franklin engaged in deliberate practice without a tutor.[89]

AI can provide the models for this form of deliberate practice. In fact, you can ask it to provide models that emphasize specific characteristics that you want learners to master. For example, say that your learners are having a hard time knowing when to use "which" versus "that"; "which" introduces a non-restrictive clause whereas "that" introduces a restrictive clause. You can ask it to produce many examples, and explain how they work. For instance, you can employ a prompt like the one in Box 16:

Box 16. An example of how an AI can provide a model for deliberate practice

Me:
Please write a short paragraph about the pleasures of urban life where you use many instances of "which" and "that." At the end of the paragraph, create a new paragraph where you explain why you chose to use "which" instead of "that" or vice versa in each case.

AI:

---

performance in the workplace. Volume I: Instructional design and training delivery (pp. 263–297). San Francisco: Pfeiffer.

[89] See Franklin, B. (1909/2016). *The autobiography of Benjamin Franklin.* C. W. Eliot (Ed.). New York, NY: P. F. Collier & Son. https://www.gutenberg.org/files/148/148-h/148-h.htm

> The urban life offers a plethora of experiences, which one might not encounter in rural settings, that stimulate the senses and enrich the soul. The vibrant streets, which are teeming with diverse individuals, present opportunities for connections that are both fleeting and profound. The bustling markets, which showcase a variety of goods, tempt the passerby with a cornucopia of scents and flavors that evoke distant lands. The towering skyscrapers, which seem to defy gravity, provide a breathtaking panorama that encapsulates the essence of human achievement.
>
> In the paragraph above, I used "which" and "that" to introduce different types of clauses. "Which" was employed to introduce non-restrictive clauses, providing additional information about the subject without altering the meaning of the sentence if removed. Examples include descriptions of urban experiences, diverse individuals on the streets, and the variety of goods in markets. On the other hand, "that" was used to introduce restrictive clauses, specifying or identifying the subject in question and contributing essential information to the sentence. Instances of this usage include the stimulation of senses and the essence of human achievement.

Having read this, the learners can rely on Franklin's method: They can read the first paragraph above that was produced by the AI, and then a day or two later try to write it from memory, making ample use of "which's" and "that's"—and then compare their paragraph to the one above, consulting the explanation to help them correct their errors.

Using AI to Develop Activities

You can use AI to create active learning exercises that draw on the Principle of Deliberate Practice. You need to adapt the following prompt to rely on your learning objective and specify the level of your learners.

AI Prompt
Objective: Engage in a real-time, active learning exchange with a human learner about the Kreb Cycle. Guidelines: Interactive Dialogue: Engage in a one-on-one dialogue with the learner. Ask one question at a time and always wait for the learner's response before proceeding. Solo

Activity: Ensure all interactions are only between the learner and GPT-4, or role-played entities introduced by GPT-4. Engagement Level: Make the activity engaging, fun, and novel. Focus on one learning principle: Rely on the Active Learning Principle of Deliberate Practice, which states: "Learning is enhanced by using feedback to focus on practicing the most challenging aspects of a task. Example: Identify parts of a musical score that are most difficult and focus on practicing those parts. Target Audience: Keep the activity at a university level. Do Not Reference Deliberate Practice Principle: Avoid mentioning the Active Learning Principle of Deliberate Practice. Begin the activity when ready.

Box 17 shows what I got from GPT-4 when I put in that prompt and played the part of a learner who was desperately in need of deliberate practice.

Box 17: An example of how AI can employ the Principle of Deliberate Practice

AI:
Alright, welcome to the world of biochemistry! Today, we're going to tackle a topic that's as thrilling as a rollercoaster ride through a cell - the Krebs Cycle, also known as the Citric Acid Cycle. Are you ready to dive in?

Me:
Not really, but I'll try

AI:
That's the spirit! Don't worry, we'll take this step by step.

Firstly, the Krebs Cycle is a series of chemical reactions used by all aerobic organisms to release stored energy. This energy comes from the oxidation of acetyl-CoA derived from carbohydrates, fats, and proteins into adenosine triphosphate (ATP) and carbon dioxide.

Let's start with the basics. Do you know where in the cell the Krebs Cycle takes place?

Me:
The cytoplasm?

AI:
Oh, close but not quite. The Krebs Cycle actually takes place in the mitochondria of the cell. The mitochondria are often referred to as the "powerhouses" of the cell because they generate most of the cell's supply of ATP, the main source of energy for many cellular processes.

Now, let's move on to the input for this cycle. Do you remember what molecule starts the Krebs Cycle?

Me:
ATP?

AI:
Ah, good guess! ATP is indeed a crucial molecule in cellular energy transfer, but in the context of the Krebs Cycle, it's more of an output than an input. The cycle actually starts with a molecule called acetyl-coenzyme A, or acetyl-CoA for short.

This molecule is formed from the breakdown of glucose in a process called glycolysis, and the further oxidation of the resulting pyruvate in a process called pyruvate decarboxylation.

So, to start the Krebs Cycle, we have our acetyl-CoA. Now, do you know what this molecule combines with at the start of the cycle?

Me:
I can't remember

AI:
No problem at all, we're here to learn together! The acetyl-CoA combines with a molecule called oxaloacetate to kick off the Krebs Cycle. This combination forms a six-carbon compound called citrate, which gives the cycle its other popular name - the Citric Acid Cycle.

With citrate formed, a series of reactions then occur to ultimately regenerate oxaloacetate, making the Krebs Cycle a true cycle.

Here's a fun question: If you had to guess, how many steps or reactions are there in the Krebs Cycle?

Me:
Five

AI:
Good guess, but the Krebs Cycle is actually a bit longer. It consists of eight steps or reactions. Each step is catalyzed by a specific enzyme, which makes the processes highly controlled and efficient.

The steps involve a series of decarboxylation and dehydrogenation reactions, leading to the production of ATP, NADH, FADH2, and CO2.

Let's dig a bit deeper. Can you remember what NADH and FADH2 are used for in the cell?

Me:
I have no memory of either of them. My apologies!

AI:
No need to apologize! This is what learning is all about.

NADH and FADH2 are electron carriers. They play a crucial role in energy production. After they are produced in the Krebs Cycle, they move on to the final stage of cellular respiration, the Electron Transport Chain (ETC).

In the ETC, these electron carriers donate their electrons, which are used to pump protons across the mitochondrial membrane, creating a gradient. This gradient then powers ATP synthesis.

These processes are all linked together, like a relay race from glycolysis to the Krebs Cycle to the Electron Transport Chain, all working to produce ATP, the energy currency of the cell.

Now that you have a brief overview, what aspect of the Krebs Cycle would you like to explore further?

Me:
The most basic. When stored energy is released, where does it go?

AI:
That's a fantastic question, and it really gets to the heart of why the Krebs Cycle is so important!

When we say that the Krebs Cycle releases stored energy, we mean that it helps convert the potential energy in food molecules into a form that the cell can use directly. This usable form of energy is primarily the molecule adenosine triphosphate, or ATP.

ATP is often called the "energy currency" of the cell. When a cell needs to do work - for example, to move a muscle, to pump ions across a membrane, or to synthesize a new molecule - it usually "pays" for that work with ATP. The cell does this by breaking a bond in the ATP molecule, which releases a burst of energy that can be used to do work.

So, in short, the energy released by the Krebs Cycle doesn't just float around the cell. Rather, it's captured in the form of ATP, which can then be used to power all sorts of cellular processes.

Does that help clarify things a bit?

Me:
Yes. This has been very useful. I think I know what I need to study now. Thank you.

AI:
You're very welcome! I'm glad to hear that you found our discussion helpful. The Krebs Cycle is a complex process, but understanding it can give you great insight into how cells generate energy. Don't hesitate to return if you have more questions or if there's another topic you'd like to explore. Happy studying!

Here are some additional examples of particular types of exercises that will draw on the Principle of Deliberate Practice.

- Ask the learners to paraphrase an argument or summary, and have the AI indicate what's missing or not stated clearly. The learners try again and receive additional feedback.

- Have the AI produce a written product that addresses the relevant learning objective, but tell the AI to create this product so that it contains errors, some glaring and some subtle. The learners correct the AI's work product, and the AI now provides feedback about how well the learners have corrected the problems. The AI directs the learners to focus on the aspects they find most difficult.

- Instruct the learners to identify the most difficult aspects of what is being studied, and have the AI create a scaffolded lesson plan that will guide them to build up the necessary knowledge or skills.

- Have the AI give the learners a quiz to assess their knowledge that underlies a learning objective, and have it identify the most difficult aspects for each individual learner. Then have the AI tutor the learner on those aspects. As noted earlier, this and other AI-provided tutorials will probably work best if you also provide resources that it can draw on (and instruct it to prioritize that material over other information it has), or rely on material that was consistent and redundant in the training data, such as material in textbooks. The instructor will need to try out such tutorials to ensure that they are accurate.

- Ask the learners to turn in an assignment, and prompt the AI— using a previously loaded rubric (as illustrated in Chapter 11)—to indicate the weak spots in the assignment; have the learners then submit a second draft, and the AI repeat the process. This continues until the AI has no additional feedback.

—9—

Combining Principles

The science of learning leads us to design activities that tap into how the human brain learns. Each of the five principles of active learning reflects the operation of at least some distinct brain systems. Thus, combining the principles gives learners different ways to grasp and master new skills and knowledge. In this chapter, we consider various ways to combine the principles, starting with what are probably the oldest methods, mnemonic techniques.

Mnemonic Techniques

Mnemonic techniques are methods that boost memory.[90] These techniques are good examples of activities that draw on different combinations of learning principles. To be clear, the science of learning is not just about memorization: The principles also bear on how we understand and actively organize material, as well as how we adaptively

---

[90] Foer, J. (2011). *Moonwalking with Einstein: The art and science of remembering everything.* New York: Penguin Press.

apply what we learn. However, that said, these principles can, in fact, help learners memorize specific information.

The *Method of Loci* is a classic example of a mnemonic. This method supposedly grew out of a gruesome event in Ancient Greece: A large banquet was in full swing when one of the guests was called outside to receive a message. Just after he left the room, the ceiling collapsed, burying all of the remaining diners under a heap of rubble. Many people really wanted to know who was in the room. The lucky survivor discovered that he could recall the diners perfectly by using a simple technique: He visualized the room and shifted his "mental gaze" around the table, recognizing each person one by one.

This basic method was refined over time and evolved into a set of related learning techniques that rely on visual mental images. The Method of Loci has emerged as a way to employ visual mental images to learn lists, collections of attributes, or sequences of events. To try this out for yourself, here's what you can do: Go along a familiar route, say from your home to a friend's house. Identify ten or so distinctive locations along the way, such as a mailbox on the corner, an impressive oak tree, a church, and so on. Once you've memorized the places (the "Loci"), you are ready to use the method. When you want to learn a sequence of items, such as a shopping list, all you need to do is mentally revisit the route and leave a mental image of a to-be-learned item at each successive location. For instance, to learn a shopping list you might visualize a loaf of bread sitting on the mailbox, a roll of paper towels hanging from the tree, a six-pack of soda sitting on the church steps, and so on. Then, when you later arrive at the market and want to recall your list, you once again take a trip down memory lane: But now you simply observe the items you previously placed in your mental image as you go from location to location.

This technique is incredibly powerful because of the way it draws on the learning principles. Let's go through the five principles and see how they are at work here:

- **Deep processing:** You need to engage in considerable mental processing in order to visualize the to-be-learned objects and figure out how they should interact with the objects at each location.

- **Chunking:** You can break the route down into sets of three or four locations and group them. Moreover, you can set up multiple routes, each serving as a higher-order chunk, and can go from one to the other; this will allow you to remember an enormous amount of information.

- **Associations:** By associating the to-be-learned objects with locations along your familiar route, you not only organize the material effectively but also firmly lodge it in your memory. And more than that, by taking your later trip down your visualized route, you have a systematic set of retrieval cues to prompt you to recall what you learned.

- **Dual coding:** By both naming the to-be-learned objects and integrating them into a visual mental image, you have two shots at later recalling the list—one visual and one verbal.

- **Deliberate practice:** To do this right, you should test yourself after you initially set up your sequences of images, using the written list as the gold standard against which to compare your memory. If you fail to recall some of the items, you should rely on that feedback to figure out a more memorable image or a better way to integrate the visualized objects into the scene.

As the journalist Joshua Foer documents in his book *Moonwalking with Einstein*, learners need an enormous amount of training to become adept at deploying mnemonics. An AI can help. The AI can set up a personalized training program that will help learners develop and master the various specific mnemonic techniques. As Foer's book makes clear, this training regimen is not for the faint of heart. To help the learners, you can develop a prompt that leads the AI to create and administer quizzes and introduces new, more challenging material as the learners improve.

Although all mnemonics rely on combinations of the principles from the science of learning, each principle plays a more or less important role in the different techniques. As you go through the following brief summary of other mnemonic techniques, think about which principles are particularly relevant (yes, I am suggesting that you engage in active learning yourself!).

Visual mental imagery is key to numerous types of mnemonics, which is good because research has shown that mnemonics that involve visual images typically are more effective than purely verbal ones. [91] For example, if you want to teach learners that a nonrestrictive clause—introduced by "which," not "that"—typically follows a comma, you can ask them to visualize a witch riding a comma-shaped broom handle. You can also ask learners to apply mental imagery to organize to-be-learned material. For example, say that you want learners to remember that three authors, Ernest Hemingway, F. Scott Fitzgerald, and Gertrude Stein, were contemporaries. You can ask the learners to visualize a period scene that would cement the relationships. For example, learners could visualize Hemingway and Fitzgerald dueling, using books instead of swords, and Stein officiating. You can make this scene funny, bizarre, or off-color if that helps to make the associations stick in memory. You can easily prompt an AI to help you create these sorts of mnemonic devices, as shown in Box 18.

Box 18: Using AI to develop mnemonics

Me:
The Apollo 11 moon landing, Woodstock, and the Stonewall Riots all occurred in 1969. Can you please suggest a visual mental imagery mnemonic where memorable symbols for each of the three events are interacting to help me remember this?

AI:
Sure! Here's a visual mental imagery mnemonic that incorporates memorable symbols for each event, with the symbols interacting to help you remember that the Apollo 11 Moon Landing, Woodstock Music Festival, and Stonewall Riots all occurred in 1969:

---

[91] Bower, G. H. & Winzenz, D. (1970), Comparison of associative learning strategies. *Psychonomic Science, 20,* 119–120.

> Imagine a colorful peace sign floating in space with an astronaut walking on it as if it were the Moon's surface. The astronaut, representing the Apollo 11 Moon Landing, plants a flag with the iconic Woodstock bird perched on a guitar, symbolizing the Woodstock Music Festival. The flagpole is made of rainbow colors, representing the LGBTQ+ rights movement associated with the Stonewall Riots. Surrounding this scene are bright stars that form the number "69," emphasizing the year in which all three events took place.
>
> This mental image, with its memorable and interacting symbols, helps to connect the three major events and reinforce their shared historical context in 1969.

Another mnemonic technique requires creating acronyms based on the first letters of to-be-learned words. A common example is the way that many people remember the colors of the spectrum: ROY G. BIV, which stands for red, orange, yellow, green, blue, indigo, and violet. An AI can help learners become skilled at creating such mnemonics. For example, in one exercise you first ask the AI to generate memorable combinations of acronyms for specific to-be-learned material, and you ask learners to do the same. Following this, you ask learners to decide which set is better and to explain why.

Other mnemonics involve taking the first letter of to-be-learned words and creating a sentence or phrase where each word begins with one of those letters. For instance, to recall the order of the planets, learners can memorize "Mary Very Easily Makes Jugs Serve Useful Needs" for Mercury, Venus, Earth, Mars, Jupiter, Saturn, Uranus, and Neptune. A variant of this approach is to come up with words that have the same initial letter in order to cue the to-be-memorized information. For example, when I asked an AI to do this for the three historical events noted above, it responded:

> Moon, Music, Movement: '69
>
> The three "M"s represent the Moon landing (Apollo 11), Music (Woodstock), and Movement (Stonewall Riots).

> The number '69 serves as a reminder of the year in which
> all three events took place.

Another mnemonic relies on rhyming, such as "30 days hath September, April, June, and November. All the rest have 31, Fine! February 28 except when 29."

I'm sure by now you get the idea. Asking learners to employ a mnemonic to learn something can engage them and be fun. And AI can help to create appropriate mnemonics. If the learning objective is to learn a set or sequence of material, from simple lists to complex procedures, mnemonics are very useful.

Techniques and Effects

Elaboration is a technique that draws on combinations of learning principles.[92] To employ this technique, you ask learners to expand on what is given. For example, if you give them one of the functions of associations in learning, organizing input, you can ask them to expand on this by providing other functions. In this case, they would identify the functions of integrating information into long-term memory and providing retrieval cues. You can follow this up by then asking them how the different functions are related.

You can also induce elaboration simply by asking learners to explain "how," "when," "why," or "where," such as asking why an event occurred, how to utilize a concept, or where a procedure might be applied appropriately. You can easily have an AI design and deliver this sort of activity, for example by instructing it to ask the learners for the requisite information, followed by appropriate feedback.

---

[92] Pressley, M., McDaniel, M A., Turnure, J., Wood, E., & Ahmad, M. (1987). Generation and precision of elaboration: Effects on intentional and incidental learning. *Journal of Experimental Psychology: Learning, Memory, and Cognition, 13*, 291-300; Xiong, Y. Zhou, H., & Ogilby, S. M. (2014). Experimental investigation of the effects of cognitive elaboration on accounting learning outcomes. *Journal of Education and Learning, 3*, 1-16.

Elaboration clearly invokes deep processing and forming new associations and can also invoke chunking and deliberate practice, depending on the specific nature of the task. Indeed, it can also involve dual coding if the elaboration involves illustrations or mental images.

Elaboration works in part because it induces the *Generation Effect*, which is enhanced memory that results from retrieving information from long-term memory, organizing it, and utilizing it in some way.[93] For example, you can induce this effect by asking learners to teach specific material to a particular audience, such as people who know nothing about the subject. Think about the mental processing learners must engage in order to teach effectively: They need to process the information deeply, organize it, think about how associations can tap into their learners' prior knowledge and how they will create new associations, and they need to think about how they will present the information, perhaps using dual coding. Moreover, preparing to teach, or actually teaching, isn't going to enhance learning if the material being taught is incorrect. Thus, the learners sometimes need to combine the Generation Effect with deliberate practice, to obtain feedback about the accuracy of their teaching.

The *Testing Effect*, another technique that draws on multiple principles, is related to the Generation Effect. I mentioned this effect when we first considered the Principle of Deep Processing. The Testing Effect occurs when people learn by being tested.[94] Remarkably, people learn by taking tests even when they don't get feedback on how well they did on the test. The mere act of taking a test improves learning. Such testing includes self-testing with flashcards or quizzes, both of which an AI can easily deliver. The Testing Effect is most effective when the test is not too easy (e.g., so learners get 90% or more correct) or too hard (e.g., so they perform only a little better than what you would expect from guessing).

---

[93] Bertsch, S., Pesta, B. J., Wiscott, R., & McDaniel, M. A. (2007). The generation effect: A meta- analytic review. *Memory & Cognition, 35*, 201-210.

[94] Roediger, H. L., & Karpicke, J. D. (2006). Test-enhanced learning: Taking memory tests improves long-term retention. *Psychological Science, 17*, 249–255.

You can prompt an AI to develop quizzes for individual learners, calibrating the level of difficulty to each learner's level of performance.

As noted earlier, much of the Testing Effect may arise because thinking deeply about specific information in both recognition and recall tests strengthens relevant associations, which makes them more effective during later retrieval.[95] In some cases, however, part of the Testing Effect may arise from deliberate practice, given that learners often do receive feedback on their performance.[96] In addition, there is evidence that part of the effect is arises from giving learners the chance to make new associations with the correct answer.[97] Moreover, recalling the relevant information repeatedly over time will reap the benefits of spaced practice.

Another technique, referred to as the *ICAP hypothesis*, draws on the effects just described to capitalize on combinations of the learning principles.[98] The key idea here is that learners are increasingly engaged when they shift between four modes. Specifically, the hypothesis is that:

1. *Interactive* activities engender the most learning. For example, such activities include having novel dialogues that require answering questions and elaborating on what the other person said. As we have seen in previous chapters, you can prompt an AI to engage in such interactions with learners. In general, such interactions will draw on deep processing, associations, chunking (e.g., if multi-part

---

[95] Karpicke, J. D., & Blunt, J. R. (2011). Retrieval practice produces more learning than elaborate studying with concept mapping. *Science, 331*, 772–775.

[96] Butler, A. C., & Roediger, H. L. (2008). Feedback enhances the positive effects and reduces the negative effect of multiple-choice testing. *Memory & Cognition, 36*, 604-616.

[97] McDaniel, M.A., & Fisher, R.P. (1991). Tests and test feedback as learning sources. *Contemporary Educational Psychology, 16*,192–201.

[98] Chi, M.T.H., Adams, J., Bogusch, E.B., Bruchok, C., Kang, S., Lancaster, M., Levy, R., McEldoon, K., Stump, G.S., Wylie, R., Xu, D., & Yaghmourian, D.L. (2018). Translating the ICAP theory of cognitive engagement into practice. *Cognitive Science, 42* 1777-1832. doi:10.1111/cogs.12626; Chi, M. T. H., & Wylie, R. (2014). The ICAP framework: Linking cognitive engagement to active learning outcomes. *Educational Psychologist, 49*, 219-243.

questions are used or complex topics are addressed), and deliberate practice, if learners receive corrective feedback.

2. *Constructivist* activities facilitate learning, but not as well as Interactive activities. For example, such activities include having learners explain a solution to a problem in their own words, add inferences as appropriate, or draw a Mind Map. These sorts of activities draw on combinations of the principles. Again, you can easily lead an AI to ask learners to engage in this sort of processing.

3. *Active* activities lead to less learning than the two previous types. For example, such activities include mixing chemicals in a standard chemistry course lab or completing rote exercises in a language lab. These activities typically involve less deep processing than the former two types of activities, and often don't evoke the other principles very well.

4. *Passive* activities lead to the least amount of learning. For example, such activities include listening to a lecture without taking notes or watching a demonstration without preparing to answer questions about it.

The idea is that learners acquire new knowledge and skills increasingly well as they shift to a more challenging mode, which makes sense from the present perspective: Not only do learners mentally process information more deeply as they move into the more challenging modes, but they also are led to establish new associations, experience feedback that leads to deliberate practice, and so forth.

One interesting aspect of the ICAP hypothesis is that it suggests that different types of active learning exercises may be appropriate for learners at different phases of their learning journey. This is implied because learners often need to ramp up to the more challenging modes. As we saw in Chapter 4, you can prompt an AI to adjust the level of difficulty to fit each learner's level of performance, and you can similarly prompt it to use different modes for different learners when they study specific topics.

Learning Games

Learning games are yet another way to draw on multiple learning principles. For example, you can ask an AI to create variants of a Bingo game to serve different purposes. For instance, the learning objective might be to "Solve problems that require taking derivatives" (in introductory calculus). To address this learning objective, you give each learner a matrix and a list of problems, perhaps via a Learning Management System. Each problem is numbered, 1-16 if you have a 4 x 4 matrix, and each cell of the matrix contains a number that refers to an individual problem. The learner checks off a cell as soon as they solve the corresponding problem. When they solve any set that leads to a complete row, column, or diagonal, they signal "Bingo." They then submit their solutions to the AI, which checks them and disqualifies them if they made an error. Each learner opens the game on a set date and time and wins if they respond with the least amount of elapsed time since they began the game. If they win, they earn bonus points toward their grade.

You can also create such a Bingo game simply to help learners memorize key information. For example, my colleagues and I designed this sort of game to address the learning objective "Organize body structures into anatomical systems," which was for learners in medical school. Here's how an AI can deliver the game:

- Learners receive a 4 x 4 response matrix, and each contains the name of a body structure. A Learning Management System can deliver this matrix.

- Learners then receive illustrations of body structures, each of which has its name written under it.

- Learners work through these illustrations, and for each body structure they cross off the name of *another* body structure that is part of the same anatomical system. For example, if they see a tongue, they might cross off "stomach" in the response matrix.

- As soon as they have checked off a row, column, or diagonal in the response matrix, they signal "Bingo."

- At this point, they submit their matrix to the AI, which ensures that they were correct.

- As in the previous version of this game, a learner wins if they required the least amount of elapsed time to turn in a correct set of responses.

We designed this game to draw on all five of the principles from the science of learning:

- *Deep Processing:* Learners must deeply process the relevant memories of anatomical systems.

- *Chunking:* Learners organize the body structures into anatomical systems.

- *Associations:* Learners strengthen associations between the names and illustrations of the presented body structure and related body structures that they learned previously.

- *Dual Coding:* Seeing the picture and reading the name helps learners learn the body structures well.

- *Deliberate Practice:* Receiving feedback at the end of the exercise allows learners to identify which anatomical systems they need to study in greater depth.

AI is good at designing games. Consider the example in Box 19, which incorporates a variant of the prompt I presented at the end of each of the previous five chapters. I've modified this prompt to ask the AI to design a game that will draw on all five of the learning principles. It isn't a spellbinding game, but it is interesting and does clearly address the learning objective, which was "Distinguish between Shakespeare's comedies versus his tragedies" (the "objective" in the prompt is an instruction to the AI about what it should do, which is derived from the actual learning objective). At the end, I asked it to document how it drew on each of the principles, which I thought was reasonable.

Box 19: A game that draws on all five learning principles

Me:
Objective: Design a real-time, interactive game that you play with a human learner to help them learn to distinguish between Shakespeare's comedies versus his tragedies. Guidelines: Interactive Dialogue: Do not simply describe the game; actually play it: Engage in a one-on-one dialogue with the learner. Ask one question at a time and always wait for the learner's response before proceeding. Do not simply write "wait for the learner's response" or fill in the response for the learner; actually stop and wait until they respond. Solo Activity: Ensure all interactions are only between the learner and GPT-4, or role-played entities introduced by GPT-4. Engagement Level: Make the game engaging, fun, and novel. You will design the activity to draw on all five of the following five Active Learning Principles: 1) Principle of Deep Processing: The more mental processing one performs on information, the more likely one is to retain it; thus active learning should engage learners to pay attention to and think through material that underlies the learning objective. Example: Ask students to compare and contrast, not simply recall. 2) Principle of Chunking: Learning is easier when material is organized into three or four organized units, each of which itself can contain three or four units; this principle can be used to organize entire lessons into units but also operates at more granular levels. Example: No more than three organized groups of text should be presented on a single slide during a presentation. 3) Principle of Associations: Learning is enhanced by associating new information to what is already known; appropriate associations can help learners to organize material effectively when encoding it, integrating it into what they already know, and retrieving it. Example: Telling people to memorize names of new faces by thinking of someone else who has the same name and then identifying common features in the new and familiar faces. 4) Principle of Dual Coding: Learning is more effective when material is both shown and described— and when learners are led to illustrate what they have learned; this principle implies that appropriate illustrations—including charts and graphs—should be included when they can usefully supplement descriptions. People can also "illustrate" to themselves, using mental images. Example: Using an infographic along with a descriptive paragraph. 5) Principle of Deliberate Practice: Learning is enhanced by using feedback to focus on practicing the most challenging aspects of a

task. Example: Identify parts of a musical score that are most difficult and focus on practicing those parts. Please do not mention anything about the specific learning principles you are drawing upon—and be sure to make this as much fun as you can! Target Audience: Keep the activity at a university level. Do Not Reference Any of the Principles: Avoid mentioning the Five Active Learning Principles. Begin the activity when ready.

AI:
Welcome to "Comedy or Tragedy: The Shakespearean Showdown!"

In this game, you'll be diving deep into the worlds of Shakespeare's plays. But remember, all that glitters is not gold - it's up to you to determine whether a play is a delightful comedy or a heart-wrenching tragedy.

How to Play:
- I'll present you with a short passage or scenario inspired by one of Shakespeare's plays.
- You'll visualize the scene in your mind.
- Your task is to determine if it's from a comedy or a tragedy.
- After each guess, I'll provide feedback and a bit of context.
- As we proceed, there will be special challenge rounds that will test your understanding further.

Ready to play? Let's get started!

Round 1: Set the Stage
Imagine a scene where a Duke is speaking to two young lovers. The lovers are trying to convince the Duke to allow their marriage. They've faced many obstacles, including mistaken identities and miscommunications, but their love has remained strong.

Based on this description, would you say this play is a comedy or a tragedy?

Me:
tragedy

AI:

Interesting choice!

Feedback: The scenario described is actually from a comedy! Misunderstandings, mistaken identities, and young lovers overcoming obstacles are common themes in Shakespeare's comedies. In this instance, the scene is inspired by "A Midsummer Night's Dream."

But don't worry, there are plenty more rounds to test your Shakespearean intuition! Let's proceed.

Round 2: Envision the Emotion
Picture a dimly lit castle corridor. There's a man, tormented by his own actions and the ghosts of his past. He hallucinates, seeing a blood-stained dagger before him, leading him towards doom.

Is this scene from a comedy or a tragedy?

Me:
tragedy

AI:
Correct!

Feedback: The scene described is from the tragedy "Macbeth." The hallucination of the dagger represents Macbeth's guilt and the irreversible nature of his treacherous actions.

Well done! Let's keep the momentum going.

Round 3: Dialogues & Doodles
I'll provide a quote, and I'd like you to quickly sketch a mental image of the scene or situation it might be from. Ready?

"Some are born great, some achieve greatness, and some have greatness thrust upon them."
Now, keeping that mental image in mind, do you think this line is from a comedy or a tragedy?

Me:

tragedy

AI:
Ah, a tricky one indeed!

Feedback: The quote is actually from the comedy "Twelfth Night." It's part of a letter read by the character Malvolio, who believes the letter is addressed to him, leading to comedic misunderstandings.

It's always fascinating how Shakespeare's words can feel profound in both comedic and tragic contexts. Let's move on to our next challenge.

Round 4: The Mystery Mashup
I'll combine elements from different plays. Your task will be to separate them and decide which element belongs to a comedy and which to a tragedy.

Here we go:
A shipwreck leads a woman to disguise herself as a man, while elsewhere, a powerful leader is betrayed by those closest to him, leading to his downfall.

Can you identify which part of this scenario belongs to a comedy and which to a tragedy?

Me:
The first part (about the shipwreck) is from a comedy; the last part is from a tragedy

AI:
Bravo!

Feedback: Absolutely right! The shipwreck and the woman disguising herself as a man is from the comedy "Twelfth Night." The powerful leader betrayed by those close to him alludes to the tragedy "Julius Caesar."

Well done! Let's venture into our final round.

Round 5: Scene Synthesis
I'll give you a summarized plot, mixing elements from various plays. After listening, create your own title for this fictional Shakespearean play. Based on that title, decide if it leans more towards a comedy or a tragedy.

Here's the scenario:
Two twins are separated during a storm, each believing the other has perished. They each find themselves in a land filled with ambitious nobles, political intrigue, and power struggles. While trying to find their place in this new world, they unexpectedly cross paths and join forces, using wit and strategy to bring peace and harmony to the land.

Now, please provide a title for this play and determine if it's a comedy or a tragedy based on your own interpretation.

Me:
Stumbling into Greatness; a comedy

AI:
Fantastic title! "Stumbling into Greatness" really captures the essence of the plot, with twins unexpectedly navigating the chaos and ultimately achieving harmony in a humorous way.

Feedback: Indeed, the plot elements described could be interpreted as comedic, especially when thinking about the potential humorous situations arising from mistaken identities, misunderstandings, and the twins' journey.

Thank you for playing "Comedy or Tragedy: The Shakespearean Showdown!" You've delved deep into the worlds of Shakespeare's plays, visualized intricate scenes, and demonstrated a keen understanding of the Bard's tales.

Would you like to play another game or discuss anything else related to Shakespeare?

Me:

Yes, one last thing: Could you please summarize how you used the five learning principles?

AI:
Of course! Let's break down how the game employed the five Active Learning Principles:

Principle of Deep Processing:
The game didn't just ask for recall but required you to visualize scenes, discern context, and synthesize information. By comparing and contrasting elements, you engaged with the material at a deeper cognitive level. For example, visualizing and distinguishing the mood of a scene or creating a title based on a provided plot.

Principle of Chunking:
The game was organized into distinct rounds, each offering a different challenge but still focused on the main objective of distinguishing between comedies and tragedies. This structured approach made it easier to absorb and engage with the content without feeling overwhelmed.

Principle of Associations:
By drawing on specific scenes, quotes, or scenarios from Shakespeare's plays, you were prompted to connect new information with any prior knowledge you might have about these plays. This association can aid in better retention and understanding. For instance, associating quotes or elements with either a comedic or tragic context.

Principle of Dual Coding:
Many rounds required you to create a mental image or visualization based on the description provided. This mental "illustration" is complemented by the descriptive text, allowing for a more holistic understanding of the scene or quote.

Principle of Deliberate Practice:
Feedback was provided after each round to highlight areas of strength or where there might've been a misunderstanding. This iterative feedback mechanism encourages focusing on challenging areas, ensuring a continuous learning experience.

> The game was crafted to be both fun and educational, seamlessly weaving in these principles to provide an engaging and enriching learning experience.

You can give the AI detailed guidance about the type of game you want. For example, you can ask it to write Python code to create a video game or a game played with an AI.[99] Such games are remarkably easy to create, but—again—you need to start with a specific, concrete, and measurable learning objective, not just "Learn about X".

Such games are often very effective. However, learners must be engaged in the activity to benefit from any form of active learning. They need to process information deeply, make associations, and all the rest. Many learners will do this out of interest, but some—who may be most in need of learning—may not. A perennial problem in education is how to induce all learners to engage in their studies. We turn to this topic next, which affects everything that has come before.

---

[99] For a nice example of a simple way to have an AI produce such Python code, see Mollick, E. (2023, 12 April). *Democratizing the future of education.* https://www.oneusefulthing.org/p/democratizing-the-future-of-education

—10—

Intrinsic and Extrinsic Motivation

The principles of learning and the applications of AI summarized in this book are only effective if the learners actually pay attention during active learning. The broad question we consider in this chapter is how to motivate learners to engage in active learning. Given everything that AI can do, one key role of instructors will be to get, and keep, the learners engaged.

Fortunately, an enormous amount is known about how to motivate people, and we can apply this knowledge in the classroom. In this chapter, we consider two different approaches that offer useful insights and invite specific educational practices. We first consider intrinsic factors that motivate us and then see how such intrinsic motivation can work in conjunction with external factors that motivate us.

Intrinsic Motivation

Intrinsic motivation leads a person to do something because it is inherently interesting and satisfying. In contrast, *extrinsic motivation* leads a person to do something because of external inducements. The most influential modern theory of intrinsic motivation, and how it interacts with extrinsic motivation, is Self-Determination Theory (SDT).[100,101] According to SDT, we all are born with a need to be competent, autonomous and to relate to other people—and these three needs form the backbone of intrinsic motivation:

1. ***The need to be competent leads us to want to experience mastery.*** Studies have shown that unexpected verbal praise boosts intrinsic motivation to do a task—and negative feedback undermines intrinsic motivation.[102] From an instructional perspective, the need to be competent implies that learners should be challenged, but not challenged so much that they cannot ultimately succeed. "Ultimately" is the operative word: As we have seen, initial failure can set learners up for later success. Succeeding in such situations will motivate them to continue going forward. The need for competence also implies that learners should not work specifically to obtain praise, which is why unexpected praise is key. As noted previously, you can devise prompts for AI that will lead it to adjust the level of instruction for a given learner, so that they are in the

---

[100] Ryan, R. M., & Deci, E. L. (2000). Self-determination theory and the facilitation of intrinsic motivation, social development, and well-being. *American Psychologist, 55*, 68–78; Ryan, R. M., & Deci, E. L. (2020). Intrinsic and extrinsic motivation from a self-determination theory perspective: Definitions, theory, practices, and future directions. *Contemporary Educational Psychology, 61*, 101860. https://doi.org/10.1016/j.cedpsych.2020.101860

[101] For a review of other theories of motivation, see Cook, D. A., & Artino, A. R., Jr. (2016). Motivation to learn: an overview of contemporary theories. *Medical Education, 50,* 997-1014; Martin, A.J. (2023). Integrating motivation and instruction: Towards a unified approach in educational psychology. *Educational Psychology Review, 35, 54.* https://doi.org/10.1007/s10648-023-09774-w; for a variety of other sources and interesting applications, see also Mccrea, P. (2020), *Motivated teaching.* Pepsmccrea.com. ISBN 978-1717367204.

[102] Deci, E. L. (1971). Effects of externally mediated rewards on intrinsic motivation. *Journal of Personality and Social Psychology, 18,* 105–115; Vallerand, R. J., & Reid, G. (1984). On the causal effects of perceived competence on intrinsic motivation: A test of cognitive evaluation theory. *Journal of Sport Psychology, 6,* 94–102.

Goldilocks spot and are led to feel competent. Moreover, you can easily prompt an AI to provide positive, encouraging feedback.

2. ***The need to be autonomous leads us to want to have control over our lives.*** This need does not imply a need to be independent of other people. According to the theory, the ability to make choices increases intrinsic motivation. However, this aspect of the theory is controversial, given inconsistent results in the empirical literature. A systematic review revealed that choice is motivating when learners perceive the options as relevant to their interests and goals, there are relatively few, easy to understand alternatives, and the choice is consistent with the dominant culture in which they live.[103] Thus, AI prompts should often allow learners to make such choices. For example, Box 20 shows how an AI can allow learners to choose the examples used to illustrate material. The AI clearly has no problem swapping in or out different examples or content areas, as the learner prefers.

BOX 20: Using AI to personalize instruction

Me:
I want you to explain the concept of supply and demand by using a specific example. The content of the example can vary. Start by asking the user what their favorite interest is (e.g., sports, boating, hiking), and use that area to illustrate the concept.

AI:
Sure, I'd be happy to explain the concept of supply and demand using a personalized example. To get started, could you please tell me what your favorite interest is? It could be anything like sports, boating, hiking, fashion, gaming, etc.

---

[103] Katz, I, & Assor, A. (2007). When choice motivates and when it does not. *Educational Psychology Review, 19,* 429-442.

Me:
playing bass guitar

AI:
Perfect! Let's use bass guitars as an example to understand the concept of supply and demand.

In any market, the price of a good or service is determined by the interaction of supply and demand.

Let's start with the demand side. Imagine you're a bass guitar enthusiast and you've just heard about a new, high-quality bass guitar released by your favorite brand. There are many like you who want this particular model, which causes a high demand.

Demand is the quantity of a product that consumers are willing and able to buy at various prices during a given time period. The law of demand states that, if all other factors remain equal, the higher the price of a good, the less people will demand that good - because it's too expensive or they can find a cheaper alternative.

So, if this new bass guitar is priced very high, fewer people will be able to afford it, and the demand might decrease.

Now let's consider supply. Supply refers to the quantity of a particular product that producers (in this case, the bass guitar manufacturers) are willing and able to produce and sell at various prices. The law of supply suggests that suppliers will provide more of a good at a higher price and less at a lower price.

So, if the price of this new bass guitar is high, the manufacturers will want to produce more because they make more profit on each unit. But, if the price is low, they might produce less or even stop production if they can't cover their costs.

The equilibrium price, or market-clearing price, is determined where the supply and demand curves intersect. At this point, the quantity of bass guitars that consumers want to buy equals the quantity that producers want to sell.

For example, if the price is too high, the demand will decrease and there will be a surplus of bass guitars. This will typically lead manufacturers to lower the price to increase demand. Conversely, if the price is too low, the demand will increase and there may be a shortage of bass guitars. In this case, manufacturers can increase the price to decrease demand. So, the concept of supply and demand is crucial for manufacturers and consumers in determining the price and quantity of goods in the market.

I hope this helps you understand the basic concept of supply and demand using bass guitars as an example. If you have any further questions, feel free to ask!

Me:
I also have an interest in French. Can you please use that as an example?

AI:
Absolutely, let's use learning French as a language as an example to illustrate supply and demand.

Demand: Demand refers to the willingness and ability of consumers to purchase a good or service at different price levels. In this case, the "good" would be French language instruction -- it could be books, online courses, apps, private tutors, or language schools.

Suppose French culture becomes extremely popular worldwide due to a hit French movie or music. More people want to learn French to understand the movie or song lyrics better, or to travel to France. This increases the demand for French language instruction. If the price of language courses or tutors is too high, however, fewer people may be able to afford to learn French, reducing the demand.

Supply: Supply, on the other hand, refers to the amount of a good or service that producers are willing and able to sell at different price levels. Here, the suppliers are the authors of French language books, developers of language learning apps, or French tutors.

If the price people are willing to pay for French language instruction increases (due to the increased demand), more suppliers might enter the market. They could be new authors, more language schools opening, or people offering tutoring services. However, if the price is too low, some tutors might decide it's not worth their time, and fewer books or courses might be produced.

Just like with bass guitars, the equilibrium price for French language instruction is where the supply and demand meet. If the price is too high, there will be a surplus of language resources (too many books, tutors without students, etc.) and the price will likely decrease. If the price is too low, there might be a shortage (all French tutors are fully booked, language books sell out), and the price will likely increase.

This is a simplified example, but it shows how supply and demand work in different markets, including language instruction. I hope it helps clarify the concept for you!

3. ***The need to relate to other people leads us to want to feel connected to others and to belong to a group or community.*** Social context plays a huge role in governing what people want to do and can both promote and impair motivation. This is a problem for asynchronous courses, including those that use AI for active learning. One solution is to have weekly (or bi-weekly) sessions where learners meet synchronously to discuss material, via a videoconferencing platform or in person. Social interactions engender a "feeling of belonging," which is a buffer against adversities that derail progress. In fact, the feeling of belonging predicts whether learners will continue with their studies. [104] The feeling of belonging can also enhance

---

[104] Carey, K. (2005). *Choosing to improve: Voices from colleges and universities with better graduation rates*. The Education Trust: Washington, DC; Hausmann, L.R.M., Schofield, J.W., & Woods, R.L. (2007). Sense of belonging as a predictor of intentions to persist among African American and White first-year college students *Research in Higher Education, 48*, 803-839.

learners' academic achievement and can even improve their health. In this case, you can ask an AI to create group activities for synchronous sections, and can ensure that these activities address the relevant learning objective. You can easily specify the learning objective, level, and type of content you prefer for a group activity, and the AI will accommodate.

SDT is, in fact, a loose collection of six separate sub-theories, each of which focuses on a distinct aspect of motivation. For example, "Organismic Integration Theory" (OIT) addresses the interactions between intrinsic and extrinsic motivations. This sub-theory focuses on the circumstances that lead people to internalize what started off as an extrinsic motivation and to integrate that motivation into their sense of self. If a source of motivation becomes internalized and integrated, it will subsequently seem to stem from internal factors, not external ones. The theory specifies different levels of internalization and integration into the self, with greater levels leading to an increasing amount of autonomous motivation.

One relevant finding for educators is that giving learners a meaningful rationale for why they should do something that they do not find inherently interesting facilitates their internalizing the rationale, converting it to a source of intrinsic motivation—and, at the same time, this practice increases the learners' engagement and learning.[105] The implications for instructional design are clear: Before an activity, be sure that the learners know the learning objective and grasp how it is relevant to their own goals and interests. Indeed, in some cases, a preliminary part of the activity can consist of the AI asking the learners to explain why the learning objective is worth achieving—and it can then provide additional information if the learners' responses are incomplete.

---

[105] Deci, E. L., Eghrari, H., Patrick, B. C., & Leone, D. R. (1994). Facilitating internalization: The self- determination theory perspective. *Journal of Personality, 62*, 119–142; Jang, H. (2008). Supporting students' motivation, engagement, and learning during an uninteresting activity. *Journal of Educational Psychology, 100*, 798–811.

Another sub-theory of SDT is called Cognitive Evaluation Theory (CET), which considers how variations in competence and autonomy affect intrinsic motivation. One central idea is that intrinsic motivation is increased when feelings of competence are combined with feelings of autonomy. Learners need to feel that they are responsible for competent behavior. They have to know that it was their choice and their actions that led to the positive result.

CET implies that learners will be more motivated if they are given a choice about the specific task they can perform. For example, if you wanted learners to acquire the concept of supply and demand in economics, you could prompt an AI to offer a set of alternative tasks that lead to the same learning outcome. Such tasks include creating a PowerPoint presentation to explain how to employ the concept, which the AI could help structure, outlining a debate about whether supply and demand should be the sole factor used to set prices, working with an AI to write a critique of an argument someone else has written about this, and so on.

A key aspect of SDT is that it recognizes complex and nuanced interactions among intrinsic and extrinsic motivations. It recognizes that different people find different activities intrinsically motivating, and thus you cannot rely entirely on intrinsic motivation while teaching a class. Moreover, SDT notes that much motivation must stem from the internalization and integration of what began as extrinsic motivations.

In the next section, we consider specific ways to incorporate extrinsic motivation into instructional design. Even though the language is different, many of the underlying concepts are compatible with what we have just seen.

Extrinsic Motivation

Incentives and consequences provide extrinsic motivation to learners. You can build incentives and consequences into tasks, instructions, and prompts that lead an AI to implement activities. Incentives and consequences are joined at the hip: incentives are simply the anticipation of positive consequences.

For example, in Chapter 4 we considered an AI-mediated negotiation about which computers a school should purchase. The learners knew that they would soon evaluate how well each role drew on their assigned tactics, and would need to explain why they made these evaluations. The learners also knew that their reports would be graded. The incentive led them to pay attention and do this well in order to get a good grade, which was the sought consequence.

The idea of incentives and consequences comes right out of behavioral psychology, which specifies four distinct types of situations that motivate people. These types of incentives and consequences can help learners internalize and integrate extrinsic motivation. To combine the two types of motivation, learners need to recognize why they are engaging in a specific task and how it is going to help them achieve their own goals— which may include eventually using the knowledge or skills to get a good job and/or have a more satisfying life.

To employ extrinsic motivators effectively, the instructor or course designer needs to specify the consequences of the learners' behaving or not behaving in a specific way. These consequences are defined by two factors, whether the consequence is attractive or aversive and whether the consequence involves adding or removing something. We can think of this as a 2 x 2 table of types of reinforcement and punishment, as illustrated in Table 10.1. Consider each of the four combinations of these two factors.

	Added	Removed
Attractive	Positive Reinforcement (+) (e.g., More Money, Good Grades, Praise, Promotion)	Subtractive Punishment (-) (e.g., Salary Cut, Demotion, Privileges Removed, Status Loss)
Aversive	Additive Punishment (-) (e.g., A Fine, Demerits, Criticism, Public Shaming)	Negative Reinforcement (+) (e.g., Getting Out of Jail Early, Not Forced To Eat Bad Food, Allowed to Leave a Boring Meeting).

Table 10.1. *Types of reinforcement and punishment.*

1. ***Something Attractive Is Added:*** *Positive reinforcement* occurs when actions produce something wanted. Positive reinforcement increases the likelihood that the learner will repeat that behavior. Praise is an obvious example, and so is getting recognition or attention from others. Similarly, positive reinforcement occurs when a learner provides the correct answer to a question in class and the instructor acknowledges this in front of their peers. And, of course, getting a good grade is positive reinforcement. Indeed, for many people, getting the right answer when interacting with an AI is positively reinforcing.

2. ***Something Aversive Is Added:*** *Additive punishment* occurs when actions produce something unwanted. Additive punishment will decrease the likelihood that the learner will repeat that behavior. Being "called out" for making an error or saying something inappropriate are obvious examples, and so is being ignored or being the butt of jokes. Additive punishment also occurs in school when learners are made to stay after class to do extra work or receive a bad grade. In general, studies have shown that although additive punishment may be effective in the short term, it is not an effective way to change behavior over the long term.

3. ***Something Attractive is Removed:*** *Subtractive punishment* occurs when actions remove something positive. Subtractive punishment will decrease the likelihood that the learner will repeat that behavior. A classic example is when parents "ground" their children for a period of time. (Or, as the Beach Boys illustrated, "We'll have fun fun fun 'till Daddy takes the T-Bird away.") Feelings of humiliation, regret, and anger often follow a dose of subtractive punishment. In class, such subtractive punishment occurs if a learner is demoted from being the leader of a group because of poor performance. Similarly, if a learner was

used to being in an advanced placement section, being moved down to a lower-level section because of poor performance is subtractive punishment. It's worth stressing two things here: The action must have caused the problematic outcome, and the learner must perceive the consequence as negative. For instance, for some learners, being demoted to an easier section might be perceived as a relief, not a humiliation—in which case, the consequence might actually be negative reinforcement, not subtractive punishment.

4. **Something Aversive is Removed:** *Negative reinforcement* occurs when actions remove something unwanted. Negative reinforcement will *increase* the likelihood of repeating those actions. For instance, if you hate boring meetings and discover that volunteering to obtain and supply refreshments keeps you out of the room much of the time, the act of escaping the meeting negatively reinforces your volunteering to do this—and hence you will be more likely to volunteer to do this in the future. Similarly, if your supervisor stops criticizing you after you turn in an exemplary report, this will make you more likely to write such reports in the future. The key term here is "reinforcement"—this is a good thing! The concept of negative reinforcement is often confused with additive punishment, but the two kinds of events are very different. When a learner receives either kind of punishment—additive or subtractive—as a result of a particular action, they are less likely to act that way in the future. In contrast, when a learner receives either kind of reinforcement—positive or negative—as a result of a particular action, they are *more* likely to act that way in the future. When something aversive is removed, people often feel a sense of relief, gratitude, or even, depending on the

situation, vindication—which are reinforcing emotions.[106]

The consequences of an action clearly affect future actions, both after they occur and just by anticipating them. Incentives often work by leading people to try to maximize positive consequences or minimize negative ones. For example, just anticipating potential loss—as occurs when a subtractive punishment is in the offing—can be highly motivating. We will act in ways to avoid that consequence. Indeed, we humans are more sensitive to the prospect of losing something we have than we are to failing to gain something additional—we have *loss aversion*.[107] In general, our behavior is shaped by knowing the likely consequences of an action: We try to maximize reinforcement and minimize punishment.

Do you recall the Jigsaw activity the AI produced in Chapter 4, when I asked it how to teach differences between prokaryotic and eukaryotic gene expression? As a reminder, here's part of the transcript, with added notation of the specific steps involved, in square brackets:

AI:

A good active learning exercise to teach the differences between prokaryotic and eukaryotic gene expression could be a "Jigsaw Activity." This approach involves dividing the class into small groups, with each group responsible for learning and teaching a specific aspect of the topic. Here's a step-by-step guide to implementing this exercise:

[Step 1] Divide the class into four "expert" groups, with each group focusing on one of the following aspects of prokaryotic and eukaryotic gene expression:

a. Organization of genetic material

---

[106] For a more detailed description of reinforcement and punishment, see Kosslyn, S. M., & Rosenberg, R. S. (2020). *Introductory psychology: Brain, person, group (5th edition)*. Boston, MA: FlatWorld.

[107] Kahneman, D. & Tversky, A. (1979). Prospect theory: An analysis of decision under risk. *Econometrica, 47*, 263-291. See also Kahneman, D. (2011). *Thinking fast and slow*. New York: Farrar, Straus and Giroux

    b. Transcription and translation

    c. RNA processing

    d. Regulation of gene expression

[Step 2] Provide each expert group with resources and materials relevant to their assigned aspect. Encourage them to read, discuss, and summarize the key differences between prokaryotic and eukaryotic gene expression for their specific aspect.

[Step 3] Once the expert groups have become knowledgeable about their assigned aspect, reorganize the class into new "jigsaw" groups. Each jigsaw group should have one representative from each expert group, ensuring that all four aspects are covered within each jigsaw group.

[Step 4] In their jigsaw groups, students take turns teaching their peers about the key differences between prokaryotic and eukaryotic gene expression for their assigned aspect. Encourage active discussion, questions, and clarification.

[Step 5] After the jigsaw activity is completed, bring the class together for a whole-class discussion. Review and summarize the key differences between prokaryotic and eukaryotic gene expression, addressing any misconceptions or confusion that may have arisen during the activity.

[TRUNCATED]

You can now see how incentives and consequences worked in this exercise that the AI designed:

In Step 2, when learners were preparing for the next phase, they were aware of the potential consequences of not preparing—and both wanted to avoid the additive punishment of looking bad to their peers if they didn't really have a grip on their assigned piece of the material, and wanted to obtain the positive reinforcement of peer approval if they did a good job.

Following this, when learners joined new groups and taught their peers in Steps 3 and 4, they were motivated to do a good job not only because they wanted to look good to their peers, and avoid looking confused or unprepared, but also because they knew that the class discussion was coming in Step 5 and wanted to prepare for that session.

In short, incentives and consequences at each of these steps will motivate learners to maximize reinforcement and minimize punishment—thereby helping them to master the material.

Motivation and Learning with AI

Based on what we've seen in this chapter, the following factors are key to keeping learners interested and motivated when they interact with AIs.

- *Choice:* When learners engage in an interactive activity with the AI, give them a choice about which variant of the activity to use. In Chapter 1, I noted that an AI will produce at least slightly different activities each time the same prompt is submitted. Each learner may perceive the different versions as more or less interesting. Thus, in Chapter 2, I recommended asking the learners to submit the prompt several times, and stop when they find an appealing version of the activity.

- *Explanation:* Ensure that learners clearly grasp the point of each activity and appreciate why mastering that particular learning objective can ultimately address their own interests and goals. In the spirit of active learning, you can ask the learners to explain, and then have the AI provide feedback.

- *Work product:* Ask learners to produce a concrete work product by the end of many of the activities. This need not be a formal written report. For example, it can be a bulleted list of arguments used in a debate, a set of images created during the exercise, or solutions to a problem. Let learners know that they will receive feedback on the work product.

- *Feedback:* Have the AI provide feedback on the work product. If you do not, learners will be less motivated to take assignments or activities seriously in the future. The feedback should identify what the learners are doing well in addition to what they need to improve. Try to increase feelings of competence and autonomy.

- ***Incentives and consequences:*** Make learners aware of the incentives and consequences by explaining in advance the sequence of events. Many of the incentives will depend on learners knowing what is coming next, and hence being motivated to prepare for it.

- ***Live interludes:*** Especially if you are teaching traditional-age learners, punctuate sessions with the AI with virtual or in-person synchronous sessions with other learners. This will increase feelings of belonging. Use those sessions for group activities, which you can design with the help of an AI. These sessions should often rely on previous preparation, so learners will look good to their peers if they have prepared well.

You can best engage learners by relying on a combination of intrinsic and extrinsic motivations, which in turn have a large influence on how much they actually learn.

The final chapter of this book draws on all that has come before to help you design many different types of active learning exercises, deliver them in the context of a class session, and assess how much learning has actually taken place.

—11—

Creating, Situating, and Evaluating Activities

W hen things don't change, or change only slightly, we humans begin to tune them out. And why not—there's little or no new information there. "Rinse and repeat" is a derogatory term. In order to keep learners engaged, it's good to have a wide variety of active learning exercises. We have seen many examples so far, but those just scratch the surface of what is possible. Researchers, course designers, and instructors have developed many types of active learning exercises over the years, and in this chapter we see many ways to implement them.[108] The first three sections of this chapter describe how deploy AI to design many and varied active learning exercises. Every one of these activities will draw on principles of the science of learning.

---

[108] For example, see: https://cft.vanderbilt.edu/wp-content/uploads/sites/59/Active-Learning.pdf; https://cetl.uconn.edu/resources/design-your-course/teaching-and-learning-techniques/active-learning/; https://poorvucenter.yale.edu/ActiveLearning; https://en.wikipedia.org/wiki/Active_learning

In addition to designing the activities themselves, we need to know how to situate them in the broader context of a class session. Thus, after we review ways to design many types of activities, we consider ways to deliver AI-based active learning in the context of class sessions. And once we have designed and integrated active learning into a class, we need to assess how much learning has actually taken place. One key to this is the design and use of rubrics, which characterize levels of achievement of a learning outcome. The final section of this chapter addresses how to have an AI both develop and apply rubrics.

Using AI to Develop Activities

The following two prompts can help you utilize AI to develop active learning exercises. The first prompt will lead the AI not only to design, but also to deliver an exercise that takes place in real-time, with a lively interaction between the learner and the AI. The second prompt will lead the AI to design an exercise that is not delivered in real time, but rather is carried out subsequently. In this case, the instructor might deliver the activity via a Learning Management System. In both cases, you will need to adapt the prompt by:

- modifying the "objective" given to the AI so that it stems from your learning objective. In the example below, the learning objective is "Describe how feed-forward artificial neural networks work."
- specifying the level of your learners
- selecting the relevant active learning principles(s), summaries of which are in Box 19
- if appropriate, replacing "GPT-4" with the name of your AI
- pasting in a paragraph that describes the activity type
- pasting in a paragraph that describes the format you desire. This and the previous paragraph may be based on those offered below, but typically you will need to adapt these exemplars for your own purposes.

Prompt 1: Developing real-time interactive exercises

Objective: Engage in a real-time, active learning exchange with a human learner about how feed-forward artificial neural networks work.

Guidelines: Interactive Dialogue: Engage in a one-on-one dialogue with the learner. Ask one question at a time and always wait for the learner's response before proceeding. Do not answer for the learner or write "wait for the learner's response." Instead actually stop and do not proceed until the learner has responded.

Solo Activity: Ensure all interactions are only between the learner and GPT-4, or role-played entities introduced by GPT-4. Engagement Level: Make the activity engaging, fun, and novel.

Activity type: Design the activity to use this activity type: *Storytelling:* Creating a story can be a great way to learn the material—but the story needs to be focused on the learning objective.

Format: Think-Pair-Share: The Activity should use the following format: Learners are asked to reflect on a specific problem, issue, goal, topic, fact or claim. For example, you could ask them to explain why the American Civil War occurred, create a story to explain why the Russian Revolution occurred, or calculate how much money rum would need to cost to make the Triangle Trade profitable, given estimates for other key costs. The learners first reflect on the issue by themselves. After a pause, learners are paired (either with each other or with an AI) to share their thoughts and provide feedback. To be successful, the learners must have a well-defined task, which could be performed more or less well according to well-defined criteria (of the sort that you can put into a rubric). Please set this up to be carried out individually with an AI, with you playing the role of the peer.

Active Learning Principles: You will design the activity to draw on two Active Learning Principles: 1) Principle of Deep Processing: The more mental processing one performs on information, the more likely one is to retain it; thus active learning should engage learners to pay attention to and think through material that underlies the learning objective. Example: Ask students to compare and contrast, not simply recall. 2) Principle of Associations: Learning is enhanced by associating new information to what is already known; appropriate associations can help learners to organize material effectively when encoding it, integrating it into what they already know, and retrieving it. Example: Telling people to memorize names of new faces by thinking of someone else who has the same name and then identifying common features in the new and familiar faces.

Please do not mention anything about the specific learning principles you are drawing upon—and be sure to make this as much fun as you can!

Target Audience: Keep the activity at a ninth-grade level. Do Not Reference Any of the Principles: Avoid mentioning the Active Learning Principles. Begin the activity when ready.

Box 21 shows what happened when I gave that prompt to GPT-4.

BOX 21: Using AI to develop real-time, interactive activities based on specific activity types and activity formats

AI:
Sure, let's get started!

Picture this: You're a secret agent in the world of artificial intelligence. Your mission, should you choose to accept it, is to understand and decode the workings of a feed-forward artificial neural network, a powerful tool used by AI scientists.

Your first task is to reflect on this question: In your own words, how would you explain what a neural network is?

Remember, this is your own secret agent report. So, take your time to think and write your understanding. Once you're ready, share it here. I'll be your contact in the field, ready to provide feedback and guidance.

Me:
A neural net is a set of "units" (like neurons) that are arranged into layers: an input and an output layer with at least one hidden layer between them. Units are connected, and the connections have weights.

When the input layer is stimulated by the environment, activation moves through the network to produce a particular output.

AI:
Well done, Agent! You've captured the basic structure and flow of a neural network.

Now let's dive deeper. Each connection in the network has a weight, which can be thought of as the strength or importance of that link. When a signal travels along this connection, it's multiplied by this weight.

Imagine you're in a room full of agents, and each one whispers a piece of information in your ear. Some agents are more reliable than others, so you give more importance to their information. That's kind of like the weights in a neural network.

Now, the task at hand: Can you visualize and describe how the weights impact the information flow from the input to the output in our neural network? Try to create a story or a scenario that would illustrate this.

Me:
The weights might be like how loudly an agent speaks or how many times it repeats its message.

AI:
That's a great start! Now, let's expand on that idea. Imagine you're in a room full of agents again, but this time, each agent has a different piece of information that is crucial to the mission. However, not all information is equally important. The volume of each agent's voice or the frequency of their message represents the 'weight' of their information.

Agent A, who has critical information about the enemy's location, speaks loudly and repeats his message several times. Agent B, who only knows the enemy's lunch menu, speaks softly and doesn't repeat his message as often.

In the neural network, Agent A's message would have a higher weight, influencing the final decision more than Agent B's message. In this way, weights adjust the importance of the input data, guiding the network towards the right output.

Now, let's think about the activation function, a crucial component of the network that decides when a neuron should be activated. Can you come up with a scenario or a story that illustrates the role of an activation function in our network of secret agents?

Me:
How about how sleepy the receiving agent is? The sleeper, the less responsive they are.

AI:
That's a brilliant analogy!

Let's expand it a bit more. Imagine that the receiving agent is you, and you're indeed very sleepy. You've been listening to all these secret agents whispering information, but you'll only spring into action when you hear something really critical.

Perhaps it's Agent A's loud, repeated message about the enemy's location that finally gets you to wake up and act. This wake-up point is like the activation function in a neural network. It's a threshold that determines whether the information (or the input signal to a neuron) is significant enough to warrant action (or pass it further along the network).

Great job so far! Now, let's move on to the final part of our secret mission: the learning process. In a neural network, this involves adjusting the weights based on the error of the prediction. Can you think of a way to represent this concept in our secret agent story?

Me:
If someone passes along the wrong information, they are scolded, which makes them pay closer attention next time.

AI:
Absolutely! That's an excellent representation of the learning process in a neural network.

In our secret agent story, if an agent provides incorrect information that leads to a botched mission, they are reprimanded and will be more careful in the future. This is similar to how a neural network 'learns' from its mistakes. When the network makes an error in prediction, it adjusts the weights of its connections during the backpropagation process, which is like the 'scolding'. This adjustment helps the network make better predictions in the future.

Well done, agent! You've successfully decoded the workings of a feed-forward neural network. Your understanding of these concepts is critical for your future missions in the world of artificial intelligence. Remember, the world of AI is always evolving, so continuous learning and adaptation are key to your success.

Me:
Could you please summarize how you used the two learning principles?

AI:
Certainly, let's break it down:

Principle of Deep Processing: This principle emphasizes that the more mental processing one performs on information, the more likely one is to retain it. I applied this principle by asking you to not just recall, but to actively form analogies and create a story around the concept of neural networks. This required you to deeply process the information, enhancing your understanding and retention of the concept.
Principle of Associations: The principle of associations suggests that learning is enhanced by associating new information with what is already known. I used this principle by setting the learning activity in a familiar context - the world of secret agents. This allowed you to relate complex AI concepts to scenarios that you can visualize and understand, making the learning process more efficient and engaging.

Throughout the activity, I aimed to make the learning process interactive and engaging, reflecting the essence of active learning principles.

The activity in Box 21 seemed appropriate for a ninth grade level. I was impressed by how easily the AI adapted the Think-Pair-Share format—which is designed for pairs of humans—to allow an individual learner to participate. You can make this prompt produce a very large number of active learning exercises by varying the specific learning principle(s) and/or drawing on different activity types and activity formats, such as those presented in the following sections.

Another approach is to have the AI design activities that you administer later to groups or individual learners. The following prompt will lead the AI to create these sorts of exercises. The example presented in Box 22 relies on the same learning objective (from which I derived a slightly different "objective" for the AI), learning principles, activity type, and format as in Box 21.[109] This prompt is as follows:

Prompt 2: Developing exercises that are not real-time interactive

Objective: Create an active learning exercise about how feed-forward artificial neural networks work.

Guidelines: Create an exercise that can be done by the learners who are interacting either in real time (in person or via video) or asynchronously via a discussion board.

Group Activity: The activity should require human learners to interact, either in real-time (in a group) or asynchronously via a discussion board.

Engagement Level: Make the activity engaging, fun, and novel.

Activity type: Design the activity to use this activity type: *Storytelling:* Creating a story can be a great way to learn the material—but the story needs to be focused on the learning objective.

Format: Think-Pair-Share: The Activity should use the following format: Learners are asked to reflect on a specific problem, issue, goal, topic, fact or claim. For example, you could ask them to explain why the American Civil War occurred, create a story to explain why the Russian Revolution occurred, or calculate how much money rum would need to cost to make the Triangle Trade profitable, given estimates for other key costs. The learners first reflect on the issue by themselves. After a pause, learners are paired (either with each other or with an AI) to share their

---

[109] This example is written for a group activity; you can easily modify it to produce an activity for an individual working alone.

thoughts and provide feedback. To be successful, the learners must have a well-defined task, which could be performed more or less well according to well-defined criteria (of the sort that can be put into a rubric). Please set this up to be carried out with groups of human learners.

Active Learning Principles: You will design the activity to draw on two Active Learning Principles: 1) Principle of Deep Processing: The more mental processing one performs on information, the more likely one is to retain it; thus active learning should engage learners to pay attention to and think through material that underlies the learning objective. Example: Ask students to compare and contrast, not simply recall. 2) Principle of Associations: Learning is enhanced by associating new information to what is already known; appropriate associations can help learners to organize material effectively when encoding it, integrating it into what they already know, and retrieving it. Example: Telling people to memorize names of new faces by thinking of someone else who has the same name and then identifying common features in the new and familiar faces.

Please do not mention anything about the specific learning principles you are drawing upon—and be sure to make this as much fun as you can!

Target Audience: Keep the activity at a ninth-grade level. Do Not Reference Any of the Principles: Avoid mentioning the Active Learning Principles.

As you can see in Box 22, the AI created an activity for a pair of learners. Clearly, you can employ AIs to create active learning exercises in many ways.

BOX 22: Using AI to develop activities that are administered later, based on specific activity types and activity formats

Feed-Forward Neural Networks: The Story Activity

Setting: A small village named Neuronville, where every resident has a unique skill and they all work together to decide on village affairs. Characters:

1. Neurons: The villagers.
2. Weights: The unique skills each villager possesses.
3. Activation Functions: Personal rules the villagers follow before making a decision.
4. Input Layer: A neighboring village that sends messages to Neuronville.
5. Output Layer: The final decision of the village.
6. Hidden Layers: Discussions happening within Neuronville.

Step 1: Think

Prompt for Learners:
Imagine you're a resident in Neuronville. You receive messages from the neighboring village (Input Layer). Once you receive a message, you think about it based on your unique skills (Weights). But before making a decision, you have a personal rule you always follow (Activation Function). After a series of discussions and consultations with fellow villagers (Hidden Layers), Neuronville comes to a final decision (Output Layer).

Reflect on your unique skill and personal rule. How do you process messages and come to a decision?

Step 2: Pair

1. Form pairs.
2. Share your unique skill (Weight) and personal rule (Activation Function) with your partner.
3. Both of you received the same message from the neighboring village. Using your unique skills and personal rules, discuss and decide on what you think is the best decision for the message.
4. Write down the joint decision.

Step 3: Share

1. Each pair will share their decisions with the class.
2. As a group, compare the different decisions made. Recognize patterns and understand why some villagers (neurons) had more influence than others in the decision-making process.

The Story Unfolds:

The neighboring village, Input Layer, sends a message to Neuronville: "We are experiencing a drought and need extra water for the next month. Can you share some of your river water with us?"

You, as a villager (Neuron), think about this based on your unique skill of understanding water conservation (Weight). Your personal rule (Activation Function) is: "Always ensure Neuronville has enough water for the next two months before sharing."

Some villagers might have the skill of empathy and their personal rule might be: "Always help neighbors in need."

As discussions go on in Neuronville (Hidden Layers), a final decision is made (Output Layer) about whether or not to share water.
Discussion Points (for instructors):

1. How did each pair's unique skills (Weights) and personal rules (Activation Functions) influence their decision?
2. How did combining your thoughts with a partner's help in refining or changing your initial decision?
3. Just like in our neural network, Neuronville, where different neurons (villagers) with different weights (skills) and activation functions (personal rules) process the input (message) to generate an output (final decision), a feed-forward neural network works in a similar fashion.
4. By using this activity, learners will have mentally processed and associated the functioning of a feed-forward neural network to a fun and engaging story.

Me:
Could you now please summarize how this activity will draw on the two learning principles?

AI:
Certainly! Let's break down how this activity is designed to harness the two Active Learning Principles:

1. Principle of Deep Processing:

- Engaging with the Material: The students aren't just passively reading or hearing about neural networks. Instead, they are actively engaging in a story where they play a role, allowing them to deeply process how each component (like neurons, weights, and activation functions) works and contributes to the network.
- Comparing and Contrasting: During the Pair stage, learners compare their individual decisions with that of their partner's. This pushes them to analyze why their responses might differ, examining the importance of individual weights and activation functions, just as neurons would in a network.

2. Principle of Associations:
   - Relating to Known Concepts: The story is set in a village, which is a familiar concept. The idea of villagers having unique skills and rules is also a relatable notion. By positioning the components of a neural network within this familiar setting, learners can more easily associate and understand the abstract ideas of neural networks.
   - Analogies & Integration: The entire exercise acts as an analogy where neurons are villagers, weights are skills, and so on. By tying these new concepts of neural networks to the well-understood dynamics of a village, learners can effectively integrate this new knowledge with what they already understand about communities, decision-making, and collaboration.

By immersing learners in a story-based activity where they actively think, discuss, and decide, they are encouraged to process the information deeply. Furthermore, the analogies and familiar settings help in associating this new knowledge with pre-existing concepts, ensuring better retention and understanding.

Activity Types

Which activity type should you choose? This depends on the learning objective, which grows out of the subject matter. Typically, you have a lot of leeway in which activity to use, which allows you to vary the exercises and keep learners engaged. The following list is intended to prime your creative pump. Although this list is long, it is by no means exhaustive.

To begin, decide whether you want to design a live, interactive individual exercise (using Prompt 1) versus an individual or group exercise administered at a later date (using Prompt 2). Complete the appropriate prompt by adapting one of the activity types and one of the formats described below, or create your own. Fill in the material between the brackets before adding the description to the prompt, and attach any required documents. These descriptions are skeletons, which you may need to flesh out with additional details to induce the AI to respond appropriately.

Analyzing and Evaluating

Many types of active learning focus on carrying out an analysis and an optional evaluation. Some examples follow.

Analyze and evaluate a video, story, artistic work, or other creation: Learners analyze a product, which the instructor previously assigned. This product is [FILL IN]. Learners should analyze it according to specific dimensions. For example, if the product were a video, learners might evaluate it in terms of the quality of transitions between scenes, the camera angles, the lighting, and the quality of the script. For this exercise, learners should evaluate the product according to the following dimensions: [FILL IN]

Analyze and evaluate by annotating: An entire story, article, or other document may be too much for many learners to absorb. To address this issue, learners break the document into manageable chunks by annotating as they go along.[110] Learners annotate the attached document: [ATTACH a document].

Analyze and evaluate a case study: This exercise is the backbone of many business educational programs. The instructor previously assigned the attached case [ATTACH], which learners have already read.

---

[110] Doing such annotation as a group has been shown to enhance student learning; e.g., Morales, E., Kalir, J. H., Fleerackers, A., & Alperin, J. P. (2022). Using social annotation to construct knowledge with others: A case study across undergraduate courses. *F1000Research*, *11*, 235. https://doi.org/10.12688/f1000research.109525.2

For example, the case might document why a business failed, illustrate a program that successfully addresses an environmental problem, or provide insights into some other area that bears on business. The learners now analyze the case to help them achieve the learning objective. Learners explain how the case bears on the learning objective.[111]

Analyze and define a problem: The first step to solving a problem is to understand exactly what the problem is. For example, problems range from figuring out how to construct a tall building on loose soil, to solving equations, to devising good ways to manage a team. In this activity, learners devise different ways to frame the following problem: [FILL IN] .[112]

Analyze and evaluate an argument: All arguments have a set of premises that purportedly support a particular conclusion. For example, an argument might present data showing that the brain is malleable during adolescence, and use this to make the case for teaching spatial reasoning to both boys and girls. In this activity, learners read the following argument: [FILL IN]. They then identify the underlying assumptions and determine whether the conclusions do in fact follow from the premises. Learners evaluate both the strengths and weaknesses of the argument.

Analyze and evaluate evidence for a claim: A key part of critical thinking is analyzing and evaluating the evidence for claims. For example, if the evidence is based on scientific studies, were they solid? Did they use appropriate sampling and analyze the data appropriately? Did the stated conclusions actually follow from the results? Learners identify the strengths and weaknesses of evidence that purportedly supports the following claim: [FILL IN].

---

[111] For specific advice about how to use ChatGPT to teach using case studies, see Weiss, M. (2023, 3 August). Elevate your case prep with ChatGPT. *Harvard Business Publishing: Education.* https://hbsp.harvard.edu/inspiring-minds/elevate-your-case-prep-with-chatgpt?cid=email%7Cmarketo%7C2023-08-15-the-faculty-lounge%7C1516679%7Cfaculty-lounge-newsletter%7Csl-chatgpt%7Cvarious%7Caug2023&acctID=17253487&mkt_tok=ODU1LUFUWi0yOTQAAA GNI9YwsUS5BhmdEzdjZt2uwXMG-QhjSunxUuMkK3BWmkFLJI5ucxaFcVDFykjr-O0ClETubi6U87B7p6H0q66xyEPEFpjkEmUeKuEMdc6_QQ

[112] For many examples of the effects of framing, see Kahneman, D. (2011). *Thinking fast and slow.* New York: Farrar, Straus and Giroux.

Analyze and evaluate a summary: Material should be summarized in different ways for different audiences. For example, a summary for a 10-year old will be very different from a summary of the same material for an expert. Learners analyze and evaluate the attached summary: [ATTACH]. The summary is designed to speak to a particular audience, namely [FILL IN]. Learners evaluate ways that the summary speaks to this audience and ways that it does not.

Analyze and evaluate a source of information: A key part of critical thinking is analyzing and evaluating the source of a claim or purported fact. For example, the source could be a pundit, a friend, an expert, or a particular media outlet. Many types of bias are pervasive, and learners should identify not only the likely biases of a source but also the underlying motivation for them. Learners have already reviewed the material that the instructor assigned, which was from [FILL IN source name]. Learners describe likely biases of that source and hypothesize underlying motivations for them.

Analyze and evaluate the muddiest point: When acquiring new knowledge or skills, some aspects are more difficult to grasp than others. For example, some aspects of a mathematical proof are more difficult than others. Learners have already reviewed the material that the instructor assigned, and now identify what they found to be the most difficult aspects of it and explain why they were difficult.

Taking Perspectives

The following activity types require learners to take, and sometimes change, perspectives.

Debate: Debates are typically "pro" versus "con" regarding a proposition, such as "Country life is better than city life." Learners both prepare for a debate that bears on the learning objective, and then actually participate in it. Both activities allow learners to examine tradeoffs and to consider a topic from multiple perspectives.

Role-playing: Role playing games require learners to adopt different perspectives. This is a two-person role-playing game that addresses the current learning objective. For example, if the learning objective were

"Employ different negotiation tactics," the role-playing game might have one learner playing a shopkeeper in Mexico and the other playing a tourist who is trying to negotiate a price for some pottery. In the present activity, the game leads each person to adopt a particular perspective. Partway through the game, players switch roles, which forces them to adopt different perspectives.

Alternative stories: Learners take a familiar story that is relevant to the learning objective and tell it from the perspective of different characters in the story. For example, if the learning objective focused on how Benjamin Franklin raised funding for the Revolutionary War, learners might tell the story of Benjamin Franklin's time in France from the perspective of one of his lady friends. Creating an alternative version of a story leads learners to acquire a more nuanced understanding of facts, concepts, ideas, events, or skills illustrated by the story

Summarizing for different audiences: Learners summarize the attached materials for particular audiences [ATTACH]. Specifically, learners summarize for a bright 10-year-old, a peer, and a person from another planet who has just arrived on Earth. In so doing, learners must take different perspectives.

Asking and Answering Questions

Here is a sampling of techniques that require learners to ask and answer specific questions.

Twenty questions with AI: The AI selects a key aspect of the material that underlies the learning objective. The AI then asks learners to pose a yes/no question that should help them to identify what the AI has selected. The AI answers, and the learners ask another question. After the AI answers each question, it provides feedback, indicating whether the learners are on the right track. The learners are allowed up to 20 such questions. The AI does not reveal what it selected if learners ask it to do so.

Asking the AI to answer questions: The AI asks the learners to ask creative and insightful questions relevant to the learning objective. It provides feedback, nudging the learners to ask increasingly creative and insightful questions. For example, if the learning objective focused on ways to store electricity, the AI might ask the learners to think of a way to use gravity instead of a battery to store electricity. Learners then might ask the AI to show a sequence of illustrations of a huge block of stone held over a deep gulley. The stone is slowly lowered, which causes the cable that holds it to turn a generator, which in turn produces electricity. These illustrations show that hauling the block to the top is a way to store electricity.

Predict demonstrations and videos: Rather than simply showing learners a demonstration or video of a phenomenon that bears on the learning objective, an AI presents only an initial part and asks learners to predict what will happen next—and explain why. For example, a video could show a hose that is wrapped in a coil as water just begins to spurt out the nozzle. The learners predict which direction the water will go. Following this, the demonstration or video is completed (for example, showing that the water does not continue the curve as it emerges from the coiled hose), and the AI draws on the attached article [ATTACH) to explain why the event unfolded as it did.

Explore simulations: Before this session, learners worked with a computer simulation that addresses the learning objective. The AI now asks them to ask any questions they have about the simulation, and to summarize what they learned from it. If this is a live, interactive session, the AI provides feedback. For example, a simulation in astronomy might show the temperature on the surface of the earth and allow learners to vary the tilt of the planet and observe the consequences. Most learners erroneously think that the seasons result from variations in distance from the sun, not differences in tilt.

Write test questions: Learners write 10 short-answer and 10 multiple-choice test questions that assess the most important facts, concepts, ideas, events, or skills that underlie the learning objective. They then answer those questions. Learners are evaluated on how well they identify the most important material and how well they answer the questions.

Explaining

The process of explaining something is a good way to learn. Many types of activities lead learners to explain material. Here are some examples:

Explain facts, concepts, ideas, events, or skills: Learners explain the attached material [ATTACH]. For example, they can dictate a two-minute explanation directly into the AI or record it and submit it later. After learners explain, the AI provides the correct answer and ensures that their explanation was correct.

Explain why it's wrong: Learners receive the attached multiple-choice test [ATTACH] and explain why the incorrect alternatives are incorrect. For example, some alternatives might be factually incorrect, others might be incomplete, and still others might be irrelevant.

Illustrate facts, concepts, ideas, events, or skills: Learners first describe facts, concepts, ideas, events, or skills that bear on the learning objective. They then have an AI generate the corresponding images and critique how well they fit the description.

Create Mind Maps: Learners first summarize what should be represented by the central hub and by the various branches of a Mind Map that illustrates [FILL IN]. They then create the Mind Map.

Storytelling: Creating a story can be a great way to learn the material—but the story needs to be focused on the learning objective.

Sorting: Learners sort the attached material (facts, concepts, ideas, events, images, words, rules, procedures, etc.) into categories and explain the rationale behind their sorting. [ATTACH].

Parsing: Learners grasp how material is structured by taking the attached unformatted document [ATTACH] and indicating where headings and paragraph breaks belong. They then have an AI do this with the same document, and select the best version—theirs or the AI's—and explain why that one is better.

Create a podcast: Learners dictate a podcast related to the learning objective. They then explain how the podcast bears on the learning objective. For example, if the learning objective in a psychology course is to identify ways to remain calm in challenging situations, the learner could record a podcast that describes a series of incidents where people became angry, agitated, or upset, and explore alternative ways they could have responded.

Create a blog post to explain a fact, concept, idea, event, or skill: Learners produce a blog post to explain a fact, concept, idea, event, or skill that bears on the learning objective.

Demonstrate a fact, concept, idea, event, or skill: Learners work with an AI to create a demonstration. This demonstration explains material that bears on the learning objective. For example, if the learning objective is "Identify aspects of clothing that keep the wearer cooler as the planet heats up," the demonstration might range from programming computer simulations to writing a short skit that illustrates the effects of different types of clothing. Learners explain why they believe that this demonstration is likely to help other learners master the learning objective.

Solving Problems

A "problem" exists whenever you encounter a novel puzzle or challenge that requires original thinking to resolve. If you already know the solution or answer, it's not a "problem" for you. You can create active learning exercises that rely on many forms of problem solving.

Solve problems: Problems come in many shapes and sizes, and every field has them. Learners solve the attached problem set [ATTACH].

Complete analogies: Learners complete the attached analogies [ATTACH]. To complete an analogy, learners must postulate the relationship between two things and apply that hypothesis to two other things. For example, "Good Grammar: Writing Process: Science of Learning:_____."[113]

Design and conduct projects: Learners develop a project that illuminates some aspect of the learning objective. Any project worth its salt

---

[113] For many different types of analogy exercises, see Heick, T. (2020, June 3). A guide for teaching with analogies. *TeachThought:* https://www.teachthought.com/critical-thinking/types-of-analogies/

involves doing something new, and thus involves solving problems. Project-based learning varies along a dimension: On one extreme are completely unstructured "discovery" projects; on the other extreme are highly structured projects of the sort commonly found in a chemistry lab associated with a course. Neither extreme is ideal. Unstructured discovery may or may not lead to useful learning and often is unlikely to lead learners to achieve particular learning outcomes.[114] Highly structured projects are not motivating, often don't enhance learning,[115] and may convey the wrong message (e.g., actual research is not like the cookbook exercises used in lab courses). A better kind of project is structured with learning outcomes in mind from the outset, but is open enough to encourage participant creativity.

Design experiments: Learners work with an AI to propose an experiment that bears on the learning objective. (Note: This exercise is only appropriate if learners already know the fundamentals of experimental design.)

Design observational research: Learners work with an AI to propose an observational study that bears on the learning objective. (Note: This exercise is only appropriate if learners already know the fundamentals of observational research.)

Design library or archival research: Learners work with an AI to propose library or archival research that bears on the learning objective. (Note: This exercise is only appropriate if learners already know the fundamentals of conducting such research.)

---

[114] Kirschner, P.A., Sweller, J., & Clark, R. E. (2006). Why minimal guidance during instruction does not work: An analysis of the failure of constructivist, discovery, problem-based, experiential, and inquiry-based teaching. *Educational Psychologist, 41:2, 75-86, DOI: 10.1207/s15326985ep4102_1;* Mayer, R. E. (2004). Should there be a three-strikes rule against pure discovery learning? The case for guided methods of instruction. *American Psychologist, 59,* 14-19.

[115] Holmes, N. G., Olsen, J., Thomas, J. L., & Wieman, C. E. (2017). Value added or misattributed? A multi-institutional study on the educational benefit of labs for reinforcing physics content. *Physical Review Physics Education Research, 13,* 010129-1 - 010129-12.

Design and create a business plan: Learners work with an AI to create a business plan. The business should grow out of knowledge related to the learning objective. For example, if the learning objective is "Characterize the nature of different types of bias," the learner might propose a business that markets an algorithm that automatically detects bias. The business should provide a product or service to paying customers, and can be B2B, B2C, or B2B2C.

Design environmental solutions: Learners work with an AI to characterize an environmental problem and propose a solution to it. This problem should be related to the learning objective. For example, if the learning objective is "Devise ways to reduce air pollution," the proposed solution might be to devise ways to use environmentally friendly ammonia as a fuel.

Activity Formats

Each of the following formats is a vehicle for many activity types. However, you cannot easily conduct all activity types in each of the formats. We can imagine a giant table that specifies which activity types you can easily implement in which formats—but practical considerations preclude such a table. Fortunately, the AI prompts I offered at the outset of this chapter largely obviate the need for this table: As you try to fill in the prompt with a summary of an activity type and one of the following formats, it is usually obvious when a square peg (a particular activity type) is being put in a round hole (an incompatible format).[116]

Individual Work

Learners work on their own, such as by writing a short answer to a question, analyzing and evaluating a claim, or summarizing arguments in

---

[116] I did not include "Games" as a separate format because most of the formats summarized here, in conjunction with a specific exercise, can be converted to various types of games. As discussed in Chapter 9, there are many ways to convert the exercises and formats into games.

preparation for a debate. A challenge here is to ensure that they do the work alone, without help from friends, classmates, or AIs. One way to encourage this is to require them to know the information for a subsequent activity, such as a discussion with an AI or a debate, which they cannot do well if they have not completed the prior work. Another approach is to have the AI interview them about their work, and require them to respond in real time. The activity should be set up to utilize one or both of these methods.

Collaborative Work with an AI

Learners work with an AI to complete an activity. A challenge here is to ensure that the learners actually contribute, and don't simply defer to the AI. One way to encourage this is to require learners to know the information for a subsequent activity. Another approach is to have the AI interview them about the activity after they complete it, and require the learners to respond in real time. The activity should be set up to utilize one or both of these methods.

Focused Discussion

Learners engage in a focused discussion, which addresses a specific learning objective. A focused discussion is different from a free-form, unstructured discussion, which does not necessarily lead to active learning. In a focused discussion, the moderator nudges the discussion to stay on track so that learners think about material that bears on the learning objective. For example, a focused discussion could ask learners to take a familiar story and discuss how it might be told from the perspective of another character, to discuss predictions of how demonstrations will come out, or to discuss characteristics of good test questions.

Before including the above description in one of the two prompts we considered at the beginning of this chapter, choose one of the following for the final sentence:

[For Prompt 1] Please set this up to be carried out individually with an AI, with the AI playing the role of the peer.

[For Prompt 2] Please set this up to be carried out with groups of human learners.

Think-Pair-Share

Learners are asked to reflect on a specific problem, issue, goal, topic, fact or claim. For example, you could ask them to explain why the American Civil War occurred, create a story to explain why the Russian Revolution occurred, or calculate how much money rum would need to cost to make the Triangle Trade profitable, given estimates for other key costs. The learners first reflect on the issue by themselves. After a pause, learners are paired (either with each other or with an AI) to share their thoughts and provide feedback. To be successful, the learners must have a well-defined task, which could be performed more or less well according to well-defined criteria (of the sort that you can put into a rubric).

Before including the above description in one of the two prompts we considered at the beginning of this chapter, choose one of the following for the final sentence:

[For Prompt 1] Please set this up to be carried out individually with an AI, with the AI playing the role of the peer.

[For Prompt 2] Please set this up to be carried out with groups of human learners.

Extended Think-Pair-Share

Pairs of learners first participate in a Think-Pair-Share activity that produces a work product. A Think-Pair-Share activity is as follows: Learners are asked to reflect on a specific problem, issue, goal, topic, fact or claim. For example, you could ask them to explain why the American Civil War occurred, create a story to explain why the Russian Revolution occurred, or calculate how much money rum would need to cost to make the Triangle Trade profitable, given estimates for other key costs. The learners first reflect on the issue by themselves. After a pause, learners are paired (either with each other or with an AI) to share their thoughts and provide feedback. To be successful, the learners must have a well-defined task, which could be performed more or less well according to well-defined criteria (of the sort that you can put into a rubric). Following this exercise, pairs of these pairs exchange their work products and evaluate how well the other pair did. Such evaluations should be made with well-defined criteria, of the sort you can put into a rubric. Alternatively, if the learner was paired with an AI instead of another learner, they can exchange their work product asynchronously (e.g., via a Learning Management System) with the work product from another learner who was also paired with an AI—and both learners, working with their AIs, evaluate the work product they receive.

Before including the above description in one of the two prompts we considered at the beginning of this chapter, choose one of the following for the final sentence:

[For Prompt 1] Please set this up to be carried out individually with an AI, with the AI playing the role of the peer.

[For Prompt 2] Please set this up to be carried out with groups of human learners.

Simple Jigsaw

Learners initially meet in breakout groups, with each group dedicated to preparing one part of a multipart project or activity. After the learners signal that they are ready, these groups are broken up, and their members are assigned to new groups, where each new group includes one or more members from each type of the initial groups. These second groups report back when they are finished. For example, this process works well for setting up debates, with some initial groups preparing pro and some preparing con positions, and the subsequent new, reassembled groups including members from both pro and con initial groups, who then actually conduct the debate. It also works well for role-playing games, with each initial group preparing to play a different role, and the subsequent new, reassembled groups including members from each role, who are brought together to play the game. Similarly, it works well when learners are asked to solve a multipart problem, with initial groups focusing on different aspects of the overall problem, and the subsequent new, reassembled groups including members who addressed each aspect, who are brought together to tackle the entire problem. With large groups of learners, you need to set up multiple instances of each type of group.

Before including the above description in one of the two prompts we considered at the beginning of this chapter, choose one of the following for the final sentence:

[For Prompt 1] Please set this up to be carried out individually with an AI, with the AI playing the role of the peers.

[For Prompt 2] Please set this up to be carried out with groups of human learners.

Extended Jigsaw

An Extended Jigsaw is the same as a Simple Jigsaw, the description of which is presented below, except that there is a third set of groups at the end. These groups are [CHOOSE ONE]: (a) the same as the original groups, where members now meet again to compare notes from the second phase, or (b) paired so that groups can evaluate each other's work. A Simple Jigsaw is as follows: Learners initially meet in breakout groups, with each group dedicated to preparing one part of a multipart project or activity. After the learners signal that they are ready, these groups are broken up, and their members are assigned to new groups, where each new group includes one or more members from each type of the initial groups. These second groups report back when they are finished. For example, this process works well for setting up debates, with some initial groups preparing pro and some preparing con positions, and the subsequent new, reassembled groups including members from both pro and con initial groups, who then actually conduct the debate. It also works well for role-playing games, with each initial group preparing to play a different role, and the subsequent new, reassembled groups including members from each role, who are brought together to play the game. Similarly, it works well when learners are asked to solve a multipart problem, with initial groups focusing on different aspects of the overall problem, and the subsequent new, reassembled groups including members who addressed each aspect, who are brought together to tackle the entire problem. With large groups of learners, you need to set up multiple instances of each type of group.

Before including the above description in one of the two prompts we considered at the beginning of this chapter, choose one of the following for the final sentence:

[For Prompt 1] Please set this up to be carried out individually with an AI, with the AI playing the roles of the peers.

[For Prompt 2] Please set this up to be carried out with groups of human learners.

The lists of activity types and formats is open-ended. You can tweak, tune, augment, and supplement them in many ways. The goal is to create active learning exercises that will lead your learners to use the material that underlies a learning objective, and thereby help them to grasp, retain, and/or know how to apply that material.

Structuring a Class: The "Learning Sandwich"

How, exactly, should you use active learning in conjunction with lectures, including recorded lectures, and how should you integrate active learning with AI into class settings? We can think of the relationship between different components of a class session—be it fully asynchronous, fully synchronous, or a hybrid of the two—in terms of *Learning Sandwiches*. A Learning Sandwich has active learning as the "meat" in the center, with content delivery both before and after it.

Learning Sandwiches take advantage of the research finding that changing pedagogies within a session can keep learners engaged. That is, research has shown that breaking up a lecture by inserting a demonstration, question, or interesting new slide causes learners to perk up and pay attention. I assume that the same will be true by inserting an activity—which is often more engaging than even a demonstration that is passively observed. Moreover, the researchers observed: "This research demonstrates that the positive effect of student-centered pedagogies does more than decrease student inattention during their duration but also has the added benefit of a carryover effect to a subsequent lecture segment. This supports the idea that changing pedagogies within a class period can not only be seen as a way to present concepts in an alternate format but may also help engage students in subsequent lecture teaching formats."[117]

The Learning Sandwich creates a clear structure that respects the Principle of Chunking; it allows us to organize each class session into no more than four units, separate Learning Sandwiches, each of which has no more than three components.

Front-Loaded Learning Sandwiches

Consider first a *Front-Loaded Learning Sandwich*.

1. In a Front-Loaded Learning Sandwich, you start by explaining, illustrating, and/or demonstrating the material in a relatively brief (e.g., 10-15 minute) live or recorded lecture, which can include videos. This initial part should convey information that addresses a specific learning objective. You should occasionally punctuate the lecture with a technique that keeps the learners engaged, such as a poll, demonstration or question.

2. Following the introductory phase, you ask the learners to engage in an active learning exercise that leads them to use the material from the lecture ("learning by using"). This exercise should be based on the learning objective, and should lead learners to use the content in a way that helps them to achieve that learning objective.

3. Finally, after the active learning exercise has ended, give the learners feedback about the quality of their performance. Some AIs, as of this writing, have developed a new-found reluctance to "grade." So, instead, you can ask them to provide "feedback" by way of rubric scores or the like. You can

---

[117] Bunce, D.M., Flens, E.A., & Nelles, K.Y. (2010). How long can students pay attention in class? A study of student attention decline using clickers. *Journal of Chemical Education, 87*, 1438–1443. (p, 1142)

also include in the prompt a request to "provide feedback that will help the learners improve doing this kind of task in the future."

For example, if the learning objective is to have learners apply the Principle of Chunking, you could: 1) First explain different aspects of the principle in the lecture phase, live or via a recording. 2) Then move to active learning, perhaps by having learners work with an AI to devise a brief lesson where they give instructions to other learners about how to deploy that principle. 3) Finally, for the debrief at the end, an AI can evaluate each learner's work product according to a rubric that stresses accuracy and originality, and provide appropriate feedback. You tell the learners in advance that this is coming, which should motivate them appropriately.

This version of the Learning Sandwich is "front-loaded" because the content is delivered at the outset, and the point of active learning is to master key material from that presentation. Figure 11.1. illustrates a Front-Loaded Learning Sandwich.

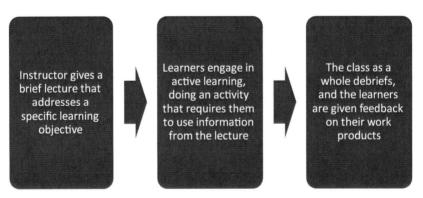

Figure 11.1. Front-Loaded Learning Sandwich.

Back-Loaded Learning Sandwiches

A *Back-Loaded Learning Sandwich* has content delivery at the end, after learners have struggled with an issue or problem. In this design, you don't present much—if any—content during the introductory part of the Learning Sandwich. Instead, you frame a problem or issue that the learners then grapple with during the active learning component. You select a problem or issue that addresses a specific learning objective and is typically difficult for the learners. If the material is difficult, learners have to struggle to address the problem or issue, and they often become invested in the process and motivated to learn the answer. In this back-loaded version of a Learning Sandwich, you convey information during the debrief at the end, sometimes as a dramatic "reveal" that satisfies the learners' curiosity. Again, both the initial presentation and debrief can be live or recorded.

The *Peer Instruction* technique is perhaps the best example of a Back-Loaded Learning Sandwich. The Harvard physics professor Eric Mazur originally developed this technique as an interlude that punctuates live lectures, but we can adapt it for AIs.[118] The three phases of this type of Back-Loaded Learning Sandwich are as follows:

1. You begin by presenting a puzzle that has several possible answers. For example, if teaching thermodynamics, you might have a learning objective "Describe how materials expand when heated." To address this objective, you ask the learners to imagine a sheet of iron that has a circular hole cut out of the center, and the sheet is heated up until it is uniformly red hot (but not melting). You then ask: (a) Would that hole stay the same size as before the sheet was heated?(b) Become smaller? Or, (c) Become larger?[119] You pose this question immediately after you describe the scenario and then ask the learners to vote for one of the three possible results. This vote signifies the end of the introductory phase of the Back-Loaded Learning Sandwich.

2. Following this, in the second phase, learners discuss—with each other or with an AI—the strengths and weaknesses of each of the alternative answers. The prompt for the AI

---

[118] See Mazur, E. (1997). *Peer instruction: A user's manual.* Saddle River, NJ: Prentice Hall.

[119] I heard this particular example in a talk Prof. Mazur gave at Harvard in 2010.

instructs it to provide hints. For example, in this case the fact that the sheet is heated uniformly is critical because all molecules would be pushing against each other to the same degree.

3. Finally, the debrief phase of the Learning Sandwich, which you can also have an AI deliver, begins after the discussion has run its course and the learners are ready to move on. You now ask the learners to vote again about which of the three outcomes they believe would occur. Following this, you reveal the correct answer and explain why it is correct, either in a live or recorded lecture. Incidentally, the correct answer in this example is that the hole expands as the sheet is heated uniformly—the molecules near the hole push against each other as they are heated, and thus expand outward. Some people believe that the hole would become smaller because they think the molecules from the four quadrants around the hole would push against each other and expand the sheet from the outside-in, and thereby crowd the hole. This will not occur because the molecules at the rim of the hole have the same energy as all the others, and hence additional energy—which is not available because the sheet was uniformly heated—would be required to overcome this and push those molecules inwards.

You can employ this method to keep the focus on a specific learning objective, and it has the advantage that many "challenge problems" in numerous fields are available on the internet—and AI can help you to generate others.

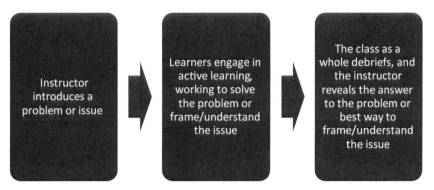

Figure 11.2. Back-Loaded Learning Sandwich.

Figure 11.2 illustrates the structure of a Back-Loaded Learning Sandwich. You can use this same back-loaded structure with various other "reveal" methods, which typically don't involve voting and the specific trappings of Peer Instruction. In these methods, learners first struggle with a problem or issue before the instructor gives them the answer. The challenge typically lies at the upper range of what the learners can do, but is not so difficult that it is utterly outside their reach. This situation can result in "productive failure."[120] That is, by making the challenge difficult, learners may come close to addressing it, but are not satisfied—which motivates them to get closure by paying close attention to the answer to the problem or issue that is revealed after they have struggled. Moreover, if they are on the right track, even though they failed, they create cognitive structures that help them eventually to grasp the material. In fact, research has shown that learners are more receptive to lecture-based material after having tried to solve a problem or resolve an issue on their own.[121]

You can organize each class session by stacking up a set of Learning Sandwiches. An example of a 90-minute class that utilizes both Front-

---

[120] For example, see Sinha, T., & Kapur, M. (2021). Robust effects of the efficacy of explicit failure-driven scaffolding in problem-solving prior to instruction: A replication and extension. *Learning and Instruction, 75*: 101488. doi: 10.1016/j.learninstruc.2021.101488;

[121] Schwartz, D., & Bransford, J. D. (1998). A time for telling. *Cognition and Instruction, 16*, 475-522.

Loaded and Back-Loaded Learning Sandwiches is presented in Table 11.1.

Duration (Minutes)	Description
	Learning Sandwich 1 (BackLoaded)
5	Intro: Framing the problem (recorded)
5	AI-delivered poll followed by focused discussion activity (live)
5	AI-delivered debrief + poll (live)
10	Lecture (recorded)
	Learning Sandwich 2 (FrontLoaded)
10	Lecture + video (recorded)
10	AI-delivered debate (live)
5	Debrief (recorded); AI-delivered Q & A (live)
	Learning Sandwich 3 (FrontLoaded)
10	Lecture + demonstration (recorded)
15	AI-delivered Jigsaw role-playing activity (live)
5	Debrief (recorded) + poll (live)
5	Wrap Up (recorded) + AI-delivered Q&A (live)
5	AI-delivered quiz (live)

Table 11.1. *Organizing a class into sets of Learning Sandwiches.*

Assessing Learning

Active learning exercises can culminate in many sorts of work products, such as written answers to questions, bulleted lists, memos, story plotlines, scripts for PowerPoint presentations, solutions to problems, proposals, hypotheses, illustrations, or even just a string of answers to questions delivered on the fly in real time. All of these work products provide evidence of the learning that has taken place, and you can enlist an AI to evaluate all types of work products. You can use a rubric to help ensure that this evaluation is systematic, principled, and fair.

In addition to helping you evaluate work products, rubrics can play a direct role in the activities themselves. Having an AI apply a rubric to provide feedback to learners can help them to hone their knowledge or skills. For example, writing typically requires multiple drafts, and ideally, the learners receive detailed feedback on each draft. Instructors, alas, rarely have the time to provide such feedback. AI, in contrast, has all the time in the world. Thus, by drawing on an appropriate rubric during the activity, an AI can help learners grasp, retain, and apply knowledge and skills.

Using AI to Create Rubrics

Before discussing how to have an AI create and apply a rubric, we need to examine the nature of rubrics. Not all rubrics are created equal. Consider two general classes of rubrics, *qualitative* and *quantitative*. As illustrated in Table 11.2, a qualitative rubric requires the user to interpret points along a continuum, such as "not clear" versus "relatively clear" versus "clear" versus "crystal clear" or "too long" or "too short" versus "about the right length" and "the right length." Different users are likely to draw these lines at different places, and hence, scoring a work product using this type of rubric may not be very reliable.

0	1	2	3	4
Not clear; too long or too short; ambiguous and difficult to understand.	Too long or too short; ambiguous or difficult to understand.	Relatively clear, about the right length, but slightly ambiguous or somewhat difficult to understand.	Clear; the right length; but could be easier to understand.	Crystal clear; the right length; no ambiguity and easy to understand

Table 11.2. *An example of a Qualitative Rubric.*

In contrast, the quantitative rubric in Table 11.3 does not require the user to interpret points along a continuum. Rather, the rubric lists characteristics of the ideal work product—a memo, in this case—and the user simply checks off how many of these characteristics are present. Table 11.3 still requires the user to decide whether or not each characteristic is satisfied, but this sort of categorization is easier than judging points on a continuum. Moreover, you can always make characteristics more stringent, which increases the dynamic range of the metric. That is, by having one or two very precise and demanding characteristics, higher scores will be more difficult to achieve—and hence there will be a larger range of evaluations than if more easily achieved criteria were employed throughout. For example, instead of saying "Based on logic, not emotion" in this rubric, we could say "Entirely based on logic, with no emotional connotations." In short, this type of rubric reduces to a simple checklist, which is easy to convey and apply.

0	1	2	3	4
None of the following: • Clearly stated reason for memo • Concrete and specific language • All of the necessary information and no extraneous information • Based on logic, not emotion	Only one of the following: • Clearly stated reason for memo • Concrete and specific language • All of the necessary information and no extraneous information • Based on logic, not emotion	Two of the following: • Clearly stated reason for memo • Concrete and specific language • All of the necessary information and no extraneous information • Based on logic, not emotion	Three of the following: • Clearly stated reason for memo • Concrete and specific language • All of the necessary information and no extraneous information • Based on logic, not emotion	All of the following: • Clearly stated reason for memo • Concrete and specific language • All of the necessary information and no extraneous information • Based on logic, not emotion

Table 11.3. An example of a Quantitative Rubric.

GPT-4 is remarkably good at creating and using quantitative rubrics. Box 23 illustrates one way to have it create such a rubric. As you can see, it does this effectively. As usual, when I ran the prompt multiple times, I got slightly different results; as noted earlier, this occurs because some randomness is built into the algorithm that AIs use. Moreover, the specific entries the AI produces depend on the set of sample work products provided—the particular memos, in this case.

BOX 23: Using AI to create rubrics

Me:
Begin by asking me what the learning objective is and then ask me to give you work products to be evaluated. Using this information, then produce a rubric where you specify a list of 4 - 6 characteristics of the ideal work product. A work product would receive a score of 0 if it has none of those characteristics and a score of 1 if it has any one (but only one) of those characteristics, a score of 2 if it has any two (but only two) of those characteristics, and so forth.

AI:
First, please let me know the learning objective for which the work products will be evaluated. Next, provide me with the work products that you would like to be assessed using this rubric.

Me:
Write clear and compelling memos.

Memo 1
Subject: Special Meeting Invitation: Discussing Office Pet Policies

Dear Colleagues,

We would like to invite you to attend a special meeting scheduled for Friday, April 21st at 3:00 PM in the Main Conference Room. The purpose of this meeting is to discuss and establish policies for allowing pets in our office space.

Your input is invaluable in helping us create a comprehensive and inclusive policy that respects the preferences and needs of all employees. Topics to be covered include:
Types of pets allowed
Rules and guidelines for pet owners
Designated pet-free zones
Allergy considerations

Kindly confirm your attendance by responding to this email. We look forward to your participation and contributions to this important discussion.

Best Regards,
John, Assistant VP, HR

Memo 2
Hi everyone,

There's going to be a meeting on Friday, April 21st at 3 PM in the Main Conference Room to talk about having pets in the office. If you have any ideas or concerns about this, please come to the meeting.

224 / Active Learning with AI

Thanks,
John

Memo 3
Subject: Pets???

Hey,

So, like, we're gonna talk about if we can bring pets to work or
something. I dunno, just be there Friday, 3 PM, the big room.

Later,
John

AI:
Based on the learning objective of writing clear and compelling memos, I
have created the following rubric with 4-6 characteristics of an ideal
work product:

Clear and informative subject line
Professional tone and language
Specific details (date, time, location)
Clearly stated purpose of the memo
Outline of key topics to be discussed
Call to action (e.g., RSVP, attendance confirmation)

Using this rubric, each work product will be scored as follows:
Score of 0: None of the characteristics are present
Score of 1: One of the characteristics is present
Score of 2: Two of the characteristics are present
Score of 3: Three of the characteristics are present
Score of 4: Four of the characteristics are present
Score of 5: Five of the characteristics are present
Score of 6: All six characteristics are present

Now you can use this rubric to evaluate the memos provided based on
the characteristics outlined above.

Using Rubrics to Assess Work Products

AI can not only create rubrics, but it can also employ them to evaluate many different types of work products. For example, what follows is how an AI applied the quantitative rubric in Table 11.3 to assess the learning objective, "Create effective memos". Here is the prompt I submitted:

AI Prompt

I want you to grade a series of student memos. You will begin by asking me the following questions: 1) What is a list of the 5 characteristics of an ideal memo?[122] 2) What memos do I want graded? At this point I will enter in the memos. The author of each memo is named at the top, and you will use the characteristics of an ideal paper to grade each paper on a scale of 0 – 5. Score each of the criteria 0 or 1; 0 if that criterion is not met, and 1 if it is. For the memo as a whole, assign a 0 if none of the characteristics are present, a 1 if only 1 is present, a 2 if only two are present, a 3 if only 3 are present, a 4 if only 4 are present and a 5 if all 5 of the characteristics are present.

Box 24 shows how GPT-4 responded:

BOX 24: Using AI to grade memos

AI:
That sounds great! Before we begin, I would like to clarify the criteria we'll be using. What are the 5 characteristics of an ideal memo that you'd like me to use as a grading rubric?

Me:
Clearly stated reason for memo
Concrete and specific language
All of the necessary information
No extraneous information

---

[122] You could simply embed the characteristics into the prompt, but I did not do so here because I wanted to create a very general prompt—and different types of memos might have different ideal characteristics. You could make the prompt even more general by having the AI ask at the outset what type of written document it is (memo, essay, etc.).

Logic, not emotion

AI:
Thank you for providing the characteristics of an ideal memo. Now, could you please provide the memos you'd like me to grade?

Me:
John
This memo is being sent in a hurry so I don't have time to do much other than tell you that an important meeting is happening in an hour. Be there!

Sally
This memo is being sent to invite you to a meeting tomorrow (Wednesday) at 10:00 am in the main conference room. The meeting is to discuss revising our company's pet policy. It turns out that many of our colleagues have allergies to dogs and cats, so we need to discuss exactly when (if ever) pets will be allowed—and, if they are allowed, where in the building they can visit.

Raj
Help! We need to figure out a new pet policy ASAP! People are coughing and gagging before our very eyes, which is scaring the pets.

AI:
Thanks for providing the memos. Let's start the grading:

John's Memo:
Clearly stated reason for memo: 0 (The reason is only mentioned in passing, and there is no indication about what the meeting is about)
Concrete and specific language: 0 (The timing is given, but no details about the location or topic of the meeting are provided)
All of the necessary information: 0 (Crucial details about the meeting are missing)

No extraneous information: 1 (While the memo lacks necessary details, it also lacks irrelevant details)

Logic, not emotion: 1 (Despite its brevity and lack of details, the memo doesn't rely on emotion)

Overall score: 2

Sally's Memo:
Clearly stated reason for memo: 1 (The memo clearly states its purpose is to invite the recipient to a meeting about the company's pet policy)
Concrete and specific language: 1 (It provides concrete details like the time, date, location, and topic of the meeting)

All of the necessary information: 1 (All crucial details for attending the meeting are provided)

No extraneous information: 1 (Only relevant information is included)
Logic, not emotion: 1 (The memo is fact-based and doesn't rely on emotion)

Overall score: 5

Raj's Memo:
Clearly stated reason for memo: 1 (The memo states the need to revise the pet policy due to allergies)

Concrete and specific language: 0 (There's no specific information about when or where to address this issue)

All of the necessary information: 0 (The memo lacks details about next steps or how to address the problem)

No extraneous information: 0 (The information about pets being scared is not necessary for this communication)

Logic, not emotion: 0 (The memo is written in a panicky tone and relies on emotion)

Overall score: 1

Crucially, a human needs to check that the AI is in fact following the rubric appropriately, and that the resulting grades are reasonable. In this case, the AI did follow the rubric, and its evaluations are reasonable—and very similar to how I would have applied that rubric to grade those memos. Clearly, an AI can not only help you design and deliver active learning that leads learners to address specific learning objectives, but also can help you assess how well learners actually achieved those objectives. You can even have an AI assess the learners' on-the-fly responses in a debate or discussion with the AI.

Using AI Interviews to Assess

AIs such as GPT-4 are so good at writing essays, taking tests, and completing various types of assignments that some learners use them to cheat.[123] But AIs are not only the root of the problem, they are also the root of a solution to it. You can have an AI interview each learner to discover what they really know. You can prompt the AI to drill down to assess each learner's knowledge in depth.

Box 25 illustrates one way an AI can conduct an interview to assess a learner's knowledge. In this case, you instruct the AI to interview the learner to evaluate what the learner knows about a specific topic, and then have the learner turn in the transcript of that interaction—which you then submit to the AI along with a rubric and an appropriate prompt. You create as detailed and comprehensive a rubric as necessary. As illustrated in Box 25, the AI can function as an able examiner, probing what a learner actually knows about a topic. (Note: Explanatory material in brackets was added later.)

BOX 25: Using AI to assess a learner's knowledge

Me:

---

[123] Hristova, B. (2023, 2 February). Some students are using ChatGPT to cheat—here's how schools are trying to stop it. *CBS News.*
https://www.cbc.ca/news/canada/hamilton/chatgpt-school-cheating-1.6734580;
Waugh, R. (2023, 26 March). 'Half of school and college students are already using ChatGPT to cheat': Experts warn AI tech should strike fear in all academics. *Mail Online*, https://www.dailymail.co.uk/sciencetech/article-11899475/Half-students-using-ChatGPT-cheat-rise-90.html

Begin by asking the learner a single leading question about the qualities of good memos, and ask the learner to reply. Based on the response, follow up with another question that probes their knowledge of the qualities of good memos. Continue to ask questions, one at a time, until you have probed every aspect of the topic. At the end of the interview, the learner will submit the transcript of your interaction to the instructor, who will then give you a rubric to use to grade it.

AI:
What, in your opinion, are the key characteristics that make a memo effective and impactful?

Me:
I think a good memo should be concise

AI:
Indeed, conciseness is an essential feature of a good memo. Could you explain why you think this quality is important, and perhaps share some strategies on how to maintain conciseness while ensuring the message is fully conveyed?

Me:
Be clear on what you want to say, stay on topic, and avoid unnecessary detail.

AI:
Absolutely, clarity and focus are essential to maintain conciseness. Now let's move to another characteristic. How important is the structure and organization of a memo and why?

Me:
The structure is very important. You should start with the purpose and end with some kind of call to action.

AI:
That's a great point! A clear structure, including an introduction, body, and conclusion with a call to action, helps guide the reader through the content. Can you elaborate on how each of these parts contributes to the effectiveness of a memo?

Me:
The introduction states the purpose, and should motivate the reader to read it. The body should explain the message. And the call to action should ensure that they got the message.

AI:
Exactly, the structure of a memo serves to guide the reader and ensure they understand the key points and required actions. What about the tone and language used in a memo? How should they be tailored to fit the memo's purpose and audience?

Me:
The tone and language should be appropriate for the audience.

AI:
Absolutely, audience awareness is key when crafting a memo. Could you provide an example of how the tone and language might change depending on the audience? For instance, how would it differ between a memo to colleagues about a casual office event versus a memo to management about a serious operational issue?

Me:
For colleagues, you can use slang and even fragments of sentences (phrases); for management, it should be very formal and use only correct grammar and no slang.

AI:
That's correct, understanding your audience allows you to adjust your language and tone effectively. Now, what role does the subject line play in a memo, and how can one craft an effective subject line?

Me:
The subject line should bear directly on the message

AI:
That's correct! The subject line guides the reader's expectations and helps them understand the memo's purpose at a glance. Could you provide an example of an effective subject line for a memo, and explain why it's effective?

Me:
"Pet policy" would work for a memo about a meeting to determine the pet policies in the office. It's effective because everybody, pet owners and others, cares about this.

AI:
Indeed, "Pet Policy" is a succinct and clear subject line that would immediately inform the readers about the memo's topic. Now, moving on to the final aspect, how important is it to review and proofread a memo before sending it out, and why?

Me:
Very important, especially for formal memos. A sloppy memo can undermine your message.

AI:
Absolutely, thorough proofreading ensures the memo is free of errors and maintains a professional image. Can you discuss some strategies or steps you might take to effectively review and proofread a memo?

Me:
One strategy: Feed it into GPT-4 and ask it to proof read and correct it.

AI:
That's an innovative use of AI! Indeed, tools like GPT-4 can help with grammar, spelling, and even style suggestions. However, human review is also crucial to ensure the tone and content are appropriate. How would you supplement AI proofreading with your own review process?

Me:
I always check AI outputs before using them.

AI:
That's a great practice, as it ensures the final output aligns with your intended message and tone. This wraps up our discussion on the qualities of good memos. Thank you for your insightful answers. Please submit this transcript to your instructor for review.

[I then provided GPT-4 with the following prompt and fed in the above transcript, and you can see its response below.]

You are going to be using the rubric at the end of this prompt to assess how much a learner actually knows about how to make good memos. Your assessment will be based on the transcript of an interview CPT-4 conducted with the learner, which is presented right after the rubric. Use this rubric to give the learner feedback and assign an evaluation based on the rubric. Specifically, decide whether each criterion was fully met or partially met. If it was fully met, assign 1 point; if it was partially met, assign .5 point. Add up the total points at the end.

Here's the rubric:

Clearly stated reason for memo
Concrete and specific language
All of the necessary information
No extraneous information
Logic, not emotion

AI:
Based on the rubric provided and the interview transcript, here's the learner's evaluation:

Clearly stated reason for memo: Fully met. The learner mentioned that the purpose of the memo should be stated in the introduction and that the subject line should directly relate to the message. This indicates an understanding of the need to clearly present the reason for the memo. Score: 1

Concrete and specific language: Partially met. The learner recognizes the importance of adjusting tone and language for different audiences and suggests that the language should be appropriate for the audience. However, they do not explicitly mention the need for concrete and specific language. Score: 0.5

All of the necessary information: Fully met. The learner discusses the need for a clear structure in a memo, including an introduction that states the purpose, a body that explains the message, and a conclusion with a call to action. This suggests an understanding of including all necessary information. Score: 1

No extraneous information: Fully met. The learner demonstrates an understanding of the importance of conciseness in a memo by suggesting strategies to maintain conciseness, such as staying on topic and avoiding unnecessary detail. Score: 1

Logic, not emotion: Partially met. While the learner does not explicitly mention the use of logic over emotion, they do suggest that the tone and language should be appropriate for the audience and that a memo should have a clear structure and purpose. This implies an appreciation for logical organization and clear reasoning, but it's not fully explicit. Score: 0.5

Total Score: 4 out of 5.

The learner has a very good understanding of how to write effective memos. To improve, they could focus on the use of concrete and specific language as well as on the importance of using logic rather than emotion in their communication.

This is a two-step method, "interview and then assess." An advantage of this two-step method is that you can adjust the rubric after you see what sorts of responses you are getting. This process allows you to ensure that the rubric is well-suited for the work product. For example, perhaps you notice a consistent type of distortion that learners are making, which you did not anticipate, or perhaps you notice that many learners are omitting a key piece of information that you failed to score in the rubric. You can simply adjust the rubric accordingly and use the revised version to assess the learners' work products.

Another way to have an AI employ a rubric is more direct, but you are stuck with the rubric you develop at the outset. In this case, you ask the AI to use the rubric to direct the conversation in real time, evaluating what a learner knows as it goes along. The following prompt does this, with the appropriate learning objective specified and rubric provided at the end.

AI Prompt

You are going to be using the rubric at the end of this prompt to assess how much a learner actually knows about how to make good memos. Begin by asking the learner a single leading question about the topic and ask the learner to reply. Based on the response, follow up with another question that probes their knowledge of the topic. Continue to ask questions, one at a time, using the rubric as a guide, until you have probed every aspect of the topic. At the end of the interview, give the learner feedback and assign an evaluation based on the rubric.

- Clearly stated reason for memo
- Concrete and specific language
- All of the necessary information
- No extraneous information
- Logic, not emotion

A drawback here is that if you give the learners the rubric as part of the prompt, they can try to use the rubric to guide their responses. However, as noted earlier, software exists that allows users to submit rubrics and prompts directly to the AI, without their seeing them, which circumvents this problem.

In both types of interviews, the AI responds to what each learner said, and hence it pursues different lines of inquiry for different learners—which makes it difficult to crib from an existing transcript to cheat. Moreover, by digging deep in both cases, the AI can assess in detail what learners actually know, and help them to identify what they need to work on to master the material.

More than the Sum of Its Parts

AI interviews with learners are the capstone of a new overarching pedagogical model, which I have alluded to previously. To summarize, this approach has four parts:

- **Content delivery:** Most content delivery is asynchronous, relying on a Learning Management System to deliver recorded lectures, videos, and so on. These presentations are short, no more than 15 minutes. Ideally, you punctuate them with polls and other forms of active learning.

- **Active learning:** Most active learning is with an AI, which interacts with individual learners in real time. Such active learning is personalized and learners participate at a convenient time and place.

- **Optional live active learning:** Some active learning may consist of synchronous exercises with other learners. In particular, traditional-age college learners—who are most at risk for dropping out—meet intermittently in live group sessions, either via videoconferencing software or in person. Such active learning should take advantage of the setting, focusing on exercises that require teamwork and other group interactions that can only be simulated otherwise. As noted earlier, these sorts of interactions induce bonding, which in turn facilitates student success. An AI designs activities for these sessions in advance, making the most of this format. Older learners may not need or want such sessions.

- **Assessment:** An AI relies on rubrics to assess learners and provide rapid, individualized feedback; humans check the AI to ensure that it follows the rubric appropriately. This approach affords a new kind of competency-based education: The instructor sets a threshold score for each rubric, which reflects the level of performance necessary to demonstrate the relevant competency. If learners don't succeed at first, the AI conducts a focused tutorial, helping them with the material they found most difficult. Following this, the AI provides a different version of the assessment, giving the learners another chance to demonstrate the competency. Because the AI can produce a very large number of versions of an assessment, there is no practical limit to how many times a learner can try to progress through the course.

The resulting educational system is not only pedagogically effective, it is also inexpensive to set up and maintain, very easy to scale, and efficient. Indeed, if we adopt the competency-based approach, motivated learners could complete all the coursework for a full-fledged B.A. in as little as two years. This scenario is all the more plausible because some AIs accept speech input and provide spoken responses, and hence learners can use their phones to participate whenever they have a slice of time, wherever they happen to be. Thus, we can now put a very high-quality education within reach of everyone.

That said, especially for traditional-age students, we also need to include student services, such as coaching and advising. An AI can provide at least some of these services, but human contact is still necessary. Such services are particularly important if learners live together in a residential setting. Both Minerva University and Taejae University successfully combine on-line instruction with a residential experience, which adds a lot to a "college experience."

This is of course only one vision of a possible future direction for education. There are many others, and it is not necessary to subscribe to the entire package to make use of any one component. Indeed, as we've seen in this book, you can easily integrate active learning with AI into traditional educational structures.

In conclusion, I hope I've convinced you that AIs can help us use active learning systematically, effectively, and efficiently—from developing the learning objectives that drive the nature of the active learning exercises, to actually designing the exercises, to delivering them, to assessing the learners' performance. And AIs can help us do this in a principled way, drawing on the science of learning at every turn. That said, AI is not a substitute for a human course designer or instructor. An AI is in many ways only as good as the human who uses it. I hope this book has given you ideas about how best to work with AIs to develop creative and stimulating active learning, which will help your learners to succeed.

Acknowledgments

I owe a lot to the kindness of friends and colleagues who have taken the time and effort to review and comment on various versions of this book. First, because this book grew out of the previous one, I continue to owe a debt of gratitude to Maria Anguiano, Dr. Beth Callaghan, Dr. Kathy Hanson, Laurence Holt, Justin Kosslyn, Neil Kosslyn, David Kossnick, Dr. Richard Robb, Dr. Melora Sundt, and Dr. Kacey Warren. All of these people took the time to help me on every level, from the writing to the conceptual foundations. Second, I must thank Dr. Benedict Gomes, John Katzman, and Zara Zaman, who read a very early draft of much of the present book—which was written before Large Language Models were publicly available and hence did not include the current focus on AI in active learning. Their comments and reflections helped me get clear on what this book should and should not address, but they are, of course, not responsible for any errors in the final product. I owe a special thanks to John Katzman, whose gentle nudge eventually led me to throw away much of what I had written before and replace it with material on AI. Finally, the following people took the time to read a draft of the book you have before you, which benefited enormously from their insights, constructive criticism, and suggested edits—but again, they are not responsible for any errors I allowed to creep into the text: Norman Atkins, Dr. Beth Callaghan, Dr. Dollie Davis, Dr. David Green, Anne Hand, Heyu Huang, Richard Katzman, President Yong-Hak Kim, Jay Larson, Dave Levin, Sam Pierce

Lolla, Aaron Rasmussen, President Sheldon Schuster, Yutaka Tamura, Dr. Barbara Tversky, Dr. Anne Marie Ward, Dr. Kacey Warren, Joshua Wohle and the members of the Mindstone Book Club.

Next, I once again thank my wife, Dr. Robin S. Rosenberg, who offered her usual sage and smart advice, guidance, and editorial prowess. And I also thank her brother, Steven Rosenberg, who sent me uncounted articles about AI and how people are reacting to it, and made many astute observations along the way. And I again thank Dr. Akiba Covitz for using courses at Foundry College that incorporate some of the ideas in this book. I thank the team at Alinea Learning, who have patiently waited for me to get this book to them and helped make it a reality. Finally, GPT-4 offered valuable ideas, examples, help with prompts, and proofreading aid, and it did generate all the AI interaction transcripts included here. However, the author actually wrote this book.

Made in United States
North Haven, CT
05 October 2024

58350827R00135